LET'S LSAT!

180 TIPS FROM 180 STUDENTS ON HOW TO SCORE 180 ON *YOUR* LSAT

JACOB EREZ

WHY YOU NEED TO READ THIS BOOK

From Ancient Greek philosophers to modern-day Cornell University professors, learning in small chunks has been recognized as the most effective way to study.

Another well-known secret-sauce recipe for success is learning from multiple perspectives.

The third idea is from the legendary motivational speaker Tony Robbins: Find someone who did exactly what you want to do, and copy them.

That's what *Let's LSAT* has to offer.

Small chunks, multiple perspectives, and 180 successful tips from LSAT students you can follow and learn from.

Those three reasons come together in the one reason you need to read this book: To help you succeed on the LSAT.

So, *Let's* LSAT!

> *"Goals are like magnets. They'll attract the things that make them come true."*
>
> *— Tony Robbins*

1

DEDICATION

The politically correct answer to the question, "Are there still any jobs for lawyers?" is: "There are jobs for *good* lawyers."

That answer's fine with me. Who would want to be represented by a bad lawyer?

But when times are tough, the tough study hard and raise the bar, making "good lawyers" the standard.

This book is dedicated, therefore, to the next generation of *great lawyers*.

Jacob

ACKNOWLEDGMENTS

First and foremost, I want to thank the incredible 180 students who contributed to this book. It amazes me every time I think about how law students and lawyers are always so supportive when it comes to helping future law students and lawyers. Thanks.

Thank you to our editors, illustrators, designers, second-guessers, and encouragers, without whom this book would have been finished a year ago. ☺

Jacob

ALSO BY THE AUTHOR:

A Cadre of Experts

A CADRE OF EXPERTS
AN LSAT NOVEL

JACOB EREZ

A Cadre of Experts is an important guide for mastering the LSAT – as well as the moving story of a young woman's journey on her way to law school.

Ripe with relatable tension and a sprinkle of humor, A Cadre of Experts thoroughly details essential LSAT concepts and exam strategies, all told through the growing friendship between Alexandra and Noah as they travel the country to consult with various experts in preparation for the exam.

More than anything, Alexandra London wants to conquer the LSAT and get into a great law school.

Will she succeed?

As an average student, Alexandra's task seems insurmountable. But with the help of Noah, a successful attorney and former LSAT instructor, along with Noah's expert friends and Alexandra's relentless tenacity and laser-focused study, this unique educational-fiction reveals a path to LSAT success anyone can follow.

We are witness to the emotional roller-coaster that Alexandra rides, sharing the highs of overconfidence and the lows of discouragement that many students face along the way. We are encouraged by Alexandra's intellectual, and, just as important, emotional growth.

Start you own journey and master the LSAT together with Alexandra and Noah, and start reading A Cadre of Experts!

Available on:

amazon.com   kindle   audible.com

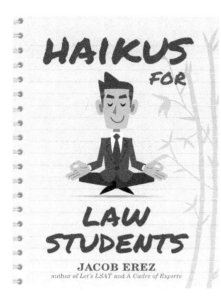

Haikus for Law Students is a collection of 105 haikus. Topics range from life as a law student to famous cases, from the grim reality of student loans and finals to clever summaries of law.

Whether you're a law student or lawyer, or buying a gift for one, Haikus for Law Students is sure to provoke a good belly laugh and provide some guilt-free entertainment.

Not defamation
when I said you're an asshole
I wasn't lying

Available on:

amazon.com   kindle   audible.com

9

CONTENTS

INTRODUCTION

O N A FLIGHT FROM SAN Francisco to New York I met Julie, an attorney. "I'm studying for the LSAT myself," I proudly told her, patting my carry-on full of LSAT books.

"That's nice," she replied, peering out the window at the houses below receding in size.

I interpreted her reply as my cue to talk. "Um, so, if you don't mind me asking, what is your advice, you know, for the LSAT?"

"You don't expect me to reveal the *real secrets* of the LSAT – not on a five-hour flight, do you?" she said with a grin. "But I *will* give you my number-one tip."

A few hours later, I was thinking about Julie's tip while waiting for my suitcase at the JFK baggage claim. As the procession of luggage started trundling down the baggage carousel, I started thinking about the zillions of lawyers and law students out there who have taken the LSAT. Then it hit me:

What if I find the top LSAT scorers and ask them for their number-one tip as well? What if I could create a book using those tips that would benefit all future LSAT students? What if I could find my suitcase and go home?

Those "what ifs" turned into the book you now hold in your hands. I hurried home and drafted the following request:

Dear law student!

We are creating a ne-of-a-kind project about the LSAT, and you can be a part of it! If you scored in the 99th percentile and would like to share your number-one tip about LSAT success with future LSAT students, please email us at… with your tips and suggestions!

Please consider any of the following subjects:

- *Logical reasoning*

- *Logic games*

- *Reading comprehension*

- *Test day*

- *Test anxiety*

- *How to study*

- *Misc.*

The more specific the better, as we are gathering quite a large number of tips.

If you need help writing your tip, consider using the following templates:

- *My tip is….*

- *I would recommend….*

- *In the specific case of….*

- *A tip that was responsible for X amount of extra points on my LSAT was….*

Your participation on this project is much appreciated. Your input will surely help countless students down the road, so, in their names, thank you!

Since then I've done a ridiculous amount of letter-writing and emailing, editing and sorting to end up with the best-quality tips. While tedious, the time I put in was well worth it. I was able to compile a huge volume of winners – 180 to be exact! This is not only a unique LSAT project – it's the only book in the world with 180 authors.

The number 180 means a lot to any LSAT student. It's the top score on the exam, one that almost guarantees acceptance into any top law school. That's why I figured 180 would be the perfect number of tips to include in this book. (I'm glad the top score isn't 2000!)

What you'll find here is a plethora of tips about various LSAT subjects. Most pertain to the LSAT sections on logical reasoning, logic games and reading comprehension, but I've also included tips on how to study, methods to improve test scores, test day, and how to deal with test anxiety.

One of the problems you might face as an LSAT student is all the contradiction and misinformation about the test on the Internet. Students have many important, pertinent questions. I took a handful of the best ones to the experts – instructors with at least five years of experience teaching the LSAT. These questions and answers can be found at the end of the book in the form of four interviews with these LSAT gurus.

This book is not designed to replace study guides, full LSAT classes or tutors. It's intended to be a supplement, with unique tips that can only be found here. (For example, "How you can master main point questions from your favorite movies," tip #56.)

This book is also useful because each tip stands alone. You don't need to read an entire chapter to benefit from it. Maximize your study time by reading a tip or two, and put some thought into them while riding the bus or subway. Take a tip and discuss it with a friend who's also studying for the LSAT. It's much easier to engage a friend in conversation if you tell him or her, "Let's talk about this tip," than if you show them a dense chapter filled with diagrams and charts and say "Looky here!"

I'm extremely proud of this book. Not because I compiled the tips, but because it proves beyond a doubt that the legal profession is a noble one. While I had tons of work to do (you should see my Starbucks bill!), the tips themselves came in quickly. Law students at top schools, eager to help, sent their tips in as soon as possible. The instructors I interviewed also were helpful with their insights, before, during, and after the interviews. They truly care about their students and their students' success on the LSAT and beyond.

I'm also proud of you for following your passion to become a lawyer. You're not taking to heart all the hype about the law profession being on an unstoppable downward spiral. You want to help people with their legal matters. You're willing to do what it takes to get into law school – and a good one, too!

"Goals are like magnets," says Tony Robbins, "They'll attract the things that make them come true." When it is time to take the LSAT, you'll be ready. When it's time to write your personal statement, you'll find just the right topics and mental images to include. Letters of recommendation? People will be fighting to write you one.

Get started with your journey: the LSAT, law school, and the legal profession. There's no journey quite like it.

Jacob Erez
July 10, 2014
New York, NY

INTRODUCTION TO THE
STUDY HABITS TIPS

T HIS FIRST SECTION IS A collection of tips that guided our top
   scorers on their journey. Imagine two people: Molly and Jane,
both traveling from North Dakota to Texas. Eager to get to their
destination, they pack maps, snacks, comic books and brand-new
sneakers. Molly is walking, but Jane is driving. Who do you think
will get to Texas first?

While both people are eager to reach their destination, it's obvious
that Jane, the one in the car, will get there sooner. Why? Because
she's using a faster means of travel.

These tips are like that. Two people can study for the LSAT. Both
may be eager, ambitious, and smart. Molly is walking, and Jane is
driving. Molly is studying, but Jane *knows how to study.* She knows
great techniques and tricks to apply to the studying process. After
reading this section, you will, too.

Jacob

TIP #1: FROM CAROL L., 176

The most important thing that comes to mind when studying for
the LSAT is to use consistent methods. When taking a prep course
with a particular company, you should not use the books or tutors

of a different one. Occasionally, there is a crossover of the methods, but mostly they clash with one another. Trying out too many is bound to lead to confusion. Friends of mine have all studied using different methods and achieved high scores. It's not the methods used as much as it is taking the time to put in the amount of work it requires to gain the skills the test demands you master.

TIP #2: FROM TAYLOR K., 177

My tip would be to study and practice the LSAT questions under different environments. The bulk of your study should take place in the library under test conditions, but practice a logic game or two on the train home. You can do simple math on the bus, right? Logic games should become as second nature as simple arithmetic, so by practicing with a noisy background, you can see how well you know the LSAT. Practice with a reading comprehension passage while walking down the street or wandering around a grocery store. Do not give up until you can get the questions right under any circumstance.

TIP #3: FROM DANIEL T., 175

You should always learn the methods of Logic Games, Logical Reasoning and Reading Comprehension before attempting the questions. Do not endeavor to solve a logic game or find an assumption in the argument without first learning the method. If you are not familiar with the correct method, you may start to adapt your own, which could be counterproductive to your study. It is hard to unlearn a habit once you have familiarized yourself with it. By studying the methods first and then approaching the questions, it will give you greater confidence and help to improve your score.

TIP #4: FROM BRIAN G., 174

My tip is to learn each of the types of question so you can recognize them quickly as soon as you see them. Simply knowing what type of game you are dealing with or what a logical reasoning question is asking you to do is very important. Then, you can apply this knowledge to real questions. This will give you a clear sense of which types of questions or games you need the most help with. This will also help you become a fast test taker.

TIP #5: FROM NATALIA R., 177

My number one tip would be to read the question stem before the stimulus. This is a must! The reason is because, once you read the question, you'll know what to look for when reading the stimulus. For example, if the question is asking you to find the assumption, you will be looking for the gap between the statement and the conclusion. Don't sit there scratching your head saying, "Wait a second. That argument doesn't make any sense." Rather, once you've noticed the gap, you'll have found the answer. Similarly, in a flaw question, if you do not read the question stem beforehand, you will get confused reading an argument that doesn't make any sense, instead of looking for the flawed reasoning as to why it doesn't make sense.

TIP #6: FROM ALEXANDRA B., 179

My strategy was to skip the hard questions and not worry about them, allowing me to make sure I got the easy questions right and then come back to the harder ones. This way I knew how much time I had left to answer the hard questions. For example, if a logical reasoning section had twenty-five questions all together and five of them were very hard, I would do the twenty easier questions first. At this point I would look at the time and see thirty minutes of this section had already passed, leaving me with one minute to answer each of the five hardest questions I left for last. While one minute may not be enough time for each question, I could still probably answer two or three before the time was up. Otherwise, if I wasted time making sure I got all the hard questions right, I might have left only twenty minutes to answer the last twenty questions. I'd much rather have one minute for each of the five difficult questions than leave myself one minute for each of the twenty easier ones.

TIP #7: FROM ESTHER H., 176

My tip is to study in two-hour increments. This way you allow yourself time to absorb the material and you don't get burned out. If you study for too long, your body gets uncomfortable and stiff; your back begins to hurt, so much so that you begin to associate the LSAT with a painful feeling. It's like when someone becomes ill after eating a bad kebab; next time they see a kebab, their body will get that same feeling of illness. Don't turn the LSAT into a bad kebab.

TIP #8: FROM PETER J., 176

At night, before you go to bed, tell yourself out loud an account of all the events of the day. Get into detail about one or two of the events. This tip is a natural way to improve your recall and memory skills, which are vital to your success on the LSAT. I saw real progress after just a week of doing this. I believe that you must work on skills outside the LSAT as well on the LSAT itself. The reason for this is that your mind needs to become stronger, change its way of thinking, the speed at which it works, as well as the amount of information it can recall. If you limit yourself to studying tests, rather than incorporating other exercises as well, it won't be as beneficial. However, if you incorporate these skills into your daily life, I believe that your mind will adapt much faster.

TIP #9: FROM MARK L., 178

My tip was something I found to be the missing link between my knowing the correct answer and my answering the question with greater speed. The link was exercise. Yes, exercise. I read that exercise would boost one's mental power by 33%. If that's the case, it should boost your LSAT score as well, I reasoned. I started working out on the treadmill, and I felt much sharper and quicker in a matter of days! (Besides the fact that I lost a few grams.) I feel very strongly about this idea. Of course, don't kid yourself that exercising will improve your score if you don't actually study, but combined with proper study, it will yield huge benefits.

TIP #10: FROM SETH G., 175

I found out about a certain idea that can help you with your LSAT study as well as improving your performance on test day. The idea is *meditation*. I saw a T-shirt that said, "Meditation is not what you think," and that is exactly the idea. You don't need any software or hardware to meditate, so don't get fooled into buying all kinds of equipment. Simply sit on your chair or on your bed in a somewhat dark and quiet room. Close your eyes and focus on how your lungs are inhaling and exhaling. If any thoughts come up, just push them aside. The idea is that it will help you concentrate, so as not to get distracted by unrelated thoughts. This is helpful in all three sections during the LSAT, but for me it was especially helpful on the reading comprehension section because I would get extremely bored and my mind would wander. After about a week of meditating 20 minutes a day, I can happily report that the problem went away, although I continued to meditate afterwards.

TIP #11: FROM SHANI T., 174

My tip is to really pay attention to what the answer choices are saying. I know this sounds obvious, but for me, it was not! I would tend to skim the answer choices looking for words that matched my idea of the correct answer. I was consistently getting around 13 out of 28 questions right until I realized my incorrect approach to the answer choices. Like I said, although it may sound like something you would be doing anyway, pay attention because you may be giving too little thought to what you are actually reading.

TIP #12: FROM JESSICA P., 177

My tip helped increase my score by ten points! You may have heard of this concept before, and I can tell you from my experience it works very well. The tip is to use the process of elimination. There are usually two to three answers that are easy to eliminate. Many times, the last two answers are somewhat similar, so you have to read carefully and look out for the details. When you get good at eliminating the wrong answers quickly, it allows you more time to decide between the two similar answers, giving you a 50/50 chance of getting it right.

TIP #13: FROM KATY Y., 177

My tip is to read the super prep LSAT book by LSAC as a preparation for your LSAT studying. While many of the study guides out there have great material, they also tend to be extremely long, whereas the super prep is concise and short mannered in giving you all the basics. I initially went through the study guides for each of the sections, but as I reviewed with super prep, I felt that it gave me the edge I needed. To take this idea a step further, try to create a cheat sheet for each of the sections. Having a quick reference to each question type can be extremely beneficial.

TIP #14: FROM ALEX H., 179

This idea is a simple one, but after all the work you put into studying for the LSAT, do not make the mistake of filling in the wrong bubbles on the answer sheet. This really would only happen in a case where you skipped an answer in order to come back to it later. For example, you answered questions 1-5 on the answer sheet. You skip question six and decide to come back to it later. Make sure you fill in question seven appropriately and not where number six should be. This is a very easy and disastrous mistake to make.

TIP #15: FROM ROY F., 174

Don't fight the LSAT because you won't win! What I mean to say is that if four out of the five answer choices seem completely wrong, and the fifth is not a completely perfect answer choice, then go with number five. Even if the answer isn't a perfect assumption, it is better than the other answers, so pick it and move on.

TIP #16: FROM ARI S., 178

How long should one study to get into the 99th percentile? That is the million-dollar question. Most of my friends that scored over

170 studied for about four months. This seems to be the right amount of time, given that you are studying for a good three hours each day. With additional time you could get better, but be careful not to burn yourself out. If you are enrolled in classes in college or you're working during this time, you may not have three quality hours to study. Do your calculations and plan to have about 240 hours of study. This does not include taking full-length LSAT tests, although reviewing them does count toward the hours.

TIP #17: FROM TERESA A., 177

I want to talk about a method that tremendously helped improve my LSAT score. I was getting every question right on single timed sections, but as soon as I tried a full practice exam, I started to miss a lot of the questions. I was used to practicing one or two sections at a time, so when it came to doing five, I was completely worn out. I decided to take it to the extreme. I started by completing one 8-section test. The physical exhaustion was quite noticeable afterwards, but the stamina I gained from it was well worth the effort. I did three more of these 8-section exams. After that, every 5-section exam was a piece of cake! I highly recommend using this method, and examples of this can be found in many sports. In baseball, for instance, a batter will practice swinging with three or even four bats before stepping up to the plate, afterwards, swinging one bat feels much easier.

TIP #18: FROM CASSANDRA S., 175

My tip is to cheer and wave your hands in the air after every answer you get right. This causes the adrenaline in your body to kick in, which in turn feels like a reward to your body. This will associate correct answers with your body feeling great. It is important to celebrate small steps and that is exactly what this does. Each correct question does in fact bring you closer to your goal, which is not to be taken for granted.

TIP #19: FROM MOE R., 176

My advice is to focus on improving the sections you are less good at. Take a real LSAT at home under test conditions. Score each section and see how you did. For example, let us say you got 20 out of 26 logical reasoning questions right, 25 out of 28 reading comprehension questions correct and 10 out of 22 logic game questions right. It's obvious in this case that you need more practice with the logic games. But how much more practice? I would advise you to split your studying in this way: spend 1/3 of your time doing logical reasoning and reading comprehension and 2/3 of your time on the logic games. Practice this for a few weeks and then take another timed LSAT at home. Perhaps it evened out; maybe you got 20 out of 23 logic game questions right, but your reading comprehension dropped to 20 out of 28. Now just adjust your time so you get more practice with the reading comprehension. Keep doing this until it evens out and then you can spend 1/3 of your time on each section.

TIP #20: FROM BLAKE O., 178

My tip is to get your logic games vocabulary down cold. Words like "precedes" or "follows" are important to understand. Precedes means to come before, so if A precedes B, that means A is before B, and if A follows B, then A is after B. This might sound like a simple thing to understand, but when you are under the stress of the test, small little words can be extremely annoying. Make flash cards for any words that you don't know perfectly, and review them before you go to sleep.

TIP #21: FROM NATHAN S., 179

My tip is to always use the actual LSAT questions! The LSAC has put many years into perfecting the questions and no LSAT tutor or company has the expertise to make up LSAT questions that would be as beneficial as the actual ones. I have a few friends who studied from books with made-up questions. I won't say the names of these books, but I will tell you that these friends of mine did not score above a 145. They told me that when they took the actual LSAT, it felt very different compared to what they had been practicing with. Besides, there are a lot of LSATs (as of today, there are 73 in print), so there really is no reason to use fake questions. You wouldn't use forged money, so don't use fake LSATs!

TIP #22: FROM CARTER H., 179

My tip is about muscle memory. What this means is that our muscles have a memory of their own. If you practice the piano, your muscles memorize the specific movements needed to make any given scale. The same goes with the logic games. Therefore, my tip is to diagram variables, diagrams, rules, etc. consistently. And it doesn't matter which way you do it. For example, if you write "not rules," such as A is not before B with an X, make sure that you always use the X. If you use a minus sign, use that minus sign all the time. This will help your hand muscles remember what to do and do them quickly.

TIP #23: FROM MILA I., 177

My tip is to practice something called Mindfulness. The idea is to keep yourself aware or mindful of certain things that we take for granted. For example, as you read this, notice your eyes. Obviously, you knew about your eyes and that you were using them, but you were probably not thinking about them consciously. Or, notice your hands, for example. Making yourself more aware of things throughout your day will help awaken your senses and intuition, and that can and will be a great help when it comes to the LSAT. On the LSAT, we read various passages, arguments, concepts, etc. But, in the need for speed, we read over important words like "most," "all," "should," "before," and "after." Reading over these words and not being mindful of them can make a huge difference in your score. If, for example, the LSAT is asking you to weaken a question, but you didn't notice that word (weaken), and are instead looking for the main point, for example, you will probably either get the question wrong or have to reread it a few times and waste valuable time.

TIP #24: FROM RILEY B., 175

If you have trouble with concentration, my tip will help. In fact, focus and concentration is the essence of the LSAT, so even if you're not bad at paying attention, you will benefit from this tip. The exercise that I want to teach you is to take two separate radios, be it a regular radio, your smart phone, etc., and listen to two different radio stations, preferably two talk shows. Now, listen to both stations simultaneously, trying to make the most of what they are each saying. After 30 seconds, turn them both off, and on paper, try to recollect what they each were about in general, any specific details mentioned, and how many speakers were speaking and the like. After a few times, up the time you do this exercise to a minute at a time. You can practice this a few minutes a day. After about an hour all together of this exercise, you will see a noticeable increase in your focus and a much stronger ability to concentrate.

TIP #25: FROM RON C., 175

My best tip for preparing for an LSAT is to understand why your incorrect answer choices are incorrect. If you don't understand why the wrong answers are incorrect, then you don't understand what they are truly saying. Chances are you will come across a correct answer choice without picking it simply because you don't understand it. The more you review your wrong answers, the faster you will be at spotting them. On test day, you really want as many weapons at your disposal as possible. The first would be the capability to spot the correct answer and a secondary capability of spotting wrong answers, so you know what not to pick.

TIP #26: FROM LUKE K., 174

If you have enough time between now and taking the LSAT, I would highly recommend dedicating two hours a week to learning new skills. Learning new skills is a highly mind-developing tool. For example, if you've never built a website, go to one of those free website builders, and build a website about a subject that you've never dealt with. This will force you to do research and boost your creativity, but the main benefit is gained from trying something new. If you make a list of ten different skills that you want to at least get a taste of, and put in a few hours into each new skill, you will develop self confidence and expand your thinking, both of which will strengthen your mind.

TIP #27: FROM MICHAEL M., 174

My tip might be a bit unusual, but in my experience it can yield wonderful results. The tip is to keep an LSAT diary. At the end of the day of your LSAT studying, write down how you felt about what you've just learned, or the details of what you've just learned. If you've noticed that a certain type of question was difficult, write that down. If you've noticed that you are faster on the logic games, write that down as well. After about two weeks of entries, you will start to notice patterns, such as you study best in the morning or at night or after exercise. You will also notice patterns about what sections you are best at. Keeping a diary is a great way to see your own progress, and that will give you motivation to continue studying and getting better at the LSAT. When your mind sees all the information on paper, it is easier for your subconscious to process it and come up with solutions for you. Try it and I am pretty certain you will be amazed.

TIP #28: FROM JAKE P., 175

I think a great tip that helped me was to use the following phrase: "It'll come to me in a second." I used that phrase – only in my head – whenever I got a little bit stuck on something. It's as if you're commanding your subconscious to come up with the answer. If you feel you are having difficulties with a specific idea, looking for the main point, the missing assumption, or an inference that is logically derived from combining two rules in a logic game; simply think to yourself, "It'll come to me in a second." It really works.

TIP #29: FROM BEN R., 178

For me, the real make it or break it point was reviewing the questions that I had already studied. Let's say you have time to get through 1000 LSAT questions throughout your study time for the LSAT. I would advocate that, instead of going over all 1000 questions once, you go over 500 of them twice. Maybe even do 250 questions four times if that works for you. Learning 250 questions and being able to recognize the patterns they have enables you to understand the arguments well, which is much better than vaguely learning 1000 questions. I'm not saying to do fewer questions; rather, I am saying to make sure that the quality of your study, or the benefit of your studying, be maximized. The LSAT tests the same things over and over again. Think of them as jokes that use the exact same punch line – they just change the variables.

LSAT Problems

INTRODUCTION TO THE
LOGICAL REASONING TIPS

T HE SECOND PART OF THIS book is dedicated to the logical
reasoning (LR) section of the LSAT. The LR is all about
arguments, but not arguments as people generally understand the
word. When people think of "arguments", they often think of their
parents arguing. However, in logic, and on the LSAT, an "argument"
is different. In the words of Wikipedia, an argument is "an attempt
to persuade someone of something, by giving reasons for accepting
a particular conclusion as evident." I believe that it is human nature
to argue in the logical sense and to want to understand the other
person's argument as well.

"But why?" is a common question from children whose parents
have just told them to go to sleep or to finish their vegetables.
"You told me to eat my veggies, but you didn't tell me why!" is
essentially like saying, "You only gave me the conclusion without
providing sufficient evidence. That, Mom and Dad, is a bad
argument." Smack!

But it's true! That would be a bad argument, and the LR section
will make you notice that. "I'm your Mother! That's why!" provides
a premise as to why a child should go to sleep. Is it a good argument?
I was brought up to believe so. (And it probably is.) As I said,
human nature is such that we want to understand another person's
argument. That's why we ask, "But why?"

Of course, the LSAT takes this to the next level. You'll need to strengthen weak arguments, find the flaws in bad arguments, bolster arguments by providing an assumption, figure out how to answer a discrepancy between two statements, and so on.

I urge you to focus on and understand all the major and minor logical fallacies. They come up again and again in the LR section. The tips here cover many of those flaws and provide an understanding of the contrapositive, formal logic, and the like. The section won't cover all the subjects covered in an LR study guide, but it provides an excellent review.

I like to think of this section as perfecting something we should all perfect. For example, I recently bought a pair of shoes. The store didn't have my size in stock, so they ordered the shoes and shipped them directly to my house. When the shoes arrived, they (of course!) were the wrong color. I checked my email, which showed that I had indeed ordered a different color than the one sent to me. The mistake was theirs, not mine. I called the store, and the manager told me I could return them, but that I'd have to pay for shipping.

What the heck?

I explained the situation to the manager. I told him that since the mistake wasn't mine, I didn't think that I should have to pay for shipping. "If it wasn't my mistake, I shouldn't have to pay for it," I argued. "Therefore, the store should cover the cost of shipping, since it was their mistake." If A, then B. Since this is clearly a case of A (as my email proved), then the outcome must be B. I thought that was solid argument. So did the manager – and he emailed me a free return label.

This might be a minor example, but my point is that you can't go through life without having to argue now and again. Otherwise, you become an easy target for scams, unjustified shoe-return costs, and emails that promise ATM cards with a million dollars in exchange for a Social Security number.

Now let me ask you this. If it wasn't for the LSAT, when else would you dedicate time and energy to learn exactly what differentiates a bad argument from a good one? Probably "one day" (meaning, never)?

So be thankful for the LR section. It might just save you money down the road.

Jacob

TIP #30: FROM MEGAN E., 177

A huge mistake people make on the logical reasoning section involves not believing the stimulus. What do I mean? If the argument tells you that all cats are gray, don't get caught up saying, "Wait a second, my cat is black! This whole stimulus is wrong!" Rather, accept the facts as true, even if you have outside knowledge that this is not the case. What you don't need to accept is the argument itself, meaning that if the conclusion doesn't follow the premise, maybe you are actually supposed to be looking for that gap in the assumption question, or a flawed reasoning in a flaw question.

TIP #31: FROM HUNTER C., 176

My advice for anybody struggling with logical reasoning is to read the book *The Duck that Won the Lottery*, by Julian Baggini. If you are new to the idea of philosophical arguments, this is a great book to get you started. I recommend reading each chapter by itself and really thinking about the ideas presented, and even trying to strike up a conversation with a friend about the topics you read about. There is no right or wrong answer, so you won't get frustrated if you don't understand everything immediately, but it will get your mind thinking in the right direction.

TIP #32: FROM ELENA R., 175

I'm sure you've heard of the negation test for necessary assumption questions. All mammals drink milk, therefore Sam drinks milk. The obvious assumption would be that Sam is a mammal. So, if you negate that by saying that Sam is not a mammal, then the argument falls apart. My tip is to use the negation test as an exercise. Practice doing assumption questions, always using the negation test, even when you are able to spot the assumption right away. This will deepen your understanding of assumptions if you practice this way on 100 or so assumption questions. On the test, however, you should, at that point, be fluent enough to spot an assumption without wasting time with the negation test.

TIP #33: FROM JULIAN A., 176

If the LSAT tells you that two things are correlated, such as the occurrence of snow storms and the selling of tea, don't assume that the way these two things are correlated are proportional. If the occurrence of snow storms goes up, that doesn't mean that the selling of tea goes up as well. It could mean that the tea sales go down, and that is their correlation – that when one goes up, the other goes down.

TIP #34: FROM CHELSEA G., 179

On must be true questions, my tip is to simply look for what supports what. Any sentence used to support another sentence is considered support, and by definition that is not the main point. Think about it like this: Why is the author of this passage presenting you with this argument? It is not in order to tell you about one simple fact that only backs up the conclusion.

TIP #35: FROM HINDY D., 178

In my opinion, *the* most important thing with the arguments is to know how to find the premise and the conclusion. However, you don't necessarily have to find them in that order; rather, you usually want to find the conclusion and then find what is supporting it. For example, it could say something like this: Baseball is a better liked sport than basketball because more tickets are sold per year for baseball games than for basketball games. So the conclusion here is that baseball is more popular, and the support, or premise, is that more tickets are sold annually for baseball. It could also appear the opposite: Since more baseball game tickets are sold each year, baseball must be more popular than basketball. Either way, the premise is the premise, and the conclusion is the conclusion, regardless of the order in which it has been presented to you.

TIP #36: FROM SAUL B., 177

For me, the arguments were all about being able to move from one argument to the next without getting caught up about in how I did on the last question. In the games and reading comprehension sections, the questions are often linked with the one before. In the arguments section, each question has absolutely nothing to do with the surrounding questions, except for the psychological effect of worrying about whether you got the previous one correct. What I did during practice exams was cover up all the text surrounding the one specific question I was working on, and I treated it like I had no other obligations except for this one question. This helped put the questions into proportion and stop me from getting nervous. Getting nervous can absolutely kill your score.

TIP #37: FROM EVAN Y., 175

For parallel reasoning questions, my tip is to look for the conclusion of the answer choices as a way to eliminate wrong answers. If the argument in the stimulus says that you should or should not do something, or that something is or isn't a certain way, you need to match that, first of all. Let's say the conclusion is that "people should exercise more." Then, you look at the answer choices and see an answer that ends with "Managers always make more money than their employees." Right away, you see that to be a wrong answer, since the conclusions don't match. "Should," is not a match of "always." In this way, you can usually eliminate at least two wrong answers, and with these long answer choices, this will save you a lot of time.

Tip #38: From Matthew T., 175

I always had an issue answering the first question correctly on the logical reasoning section. Now, that might sound a bit odd, as most of you know that the first seven or so questions are usually the easiest. Well, I also found that odd, until I realized that I was simply getting nervous about starting the section. Once I hit the second question, I was already in the groove, if you will, and things started to flow more easily from there. If this is happening to you, do what I did and simply let yourself get it wrong and make sure that you come back to it in the end. If you do not have this issue, try to discover if there are any other patterns you may have that are holding you back from getting the score you want. A tutor might be able to help in this case.

Tip #39: From Sarah Z., 177

Depending on how much time you have, you might want to look into methods that strengthen your thinking, such as brain games and the like. If you really only have a few months to study, just study LSATs and don't bother with this. However, if you have a year or so before the LSAT and you want to use your free time constructively, I would recommend a few games, such as chess, Sudoku, and my personal favorite, minesweeper. These three games help you think strategically, and they can help you with spatial reasoning as well. As far as reading comprehension goes, although the LSAT passages are unique, reading other materials like the *Economist* can help you prepare.

Tip #40: From Alyson Y., 176

When doing assumption questions, look for the gap. If the stimulus says all men are tall, therefore Max must be tall, you notice the assumption right away. Who said that Max was a man? Maybe Max is a boy. The gap occurs between the evidence (all men are tall) and the conclusion (Max must be tall). But there are sometimes tricky situations, for example: all men are tall, most tall men have a loud voice, and therefore Max must have a loud voice. Now who said that Max is a man, and who said that Max was from that majority of men with loud voices? Maybe Max is from the minority that doesn't have loud voices. The LSAT could offer you either of the assumptions as a correct answer, although never both of them as separate answers. The point here is to stay alert about what's going on in the stimulus and read all the answer choices.

TIP #41: FROM RENEE P., 179

When you approach a necessary assumption question, and you don't see a gap, look at the answer choices and find the assumption that the stimulus needs in order to make sense. For example, all bus drivers wear blue shirts. Josh wears a blue shirt. The assumption is Josh is a bus driver. But there might be an answer choice that says that Josh isn't a cab driver. Although it might be the case that Josh is only a bus driver and not a cab driver, you don't need this to be true because Josh could drive a bus and a cab, but since he drives a bus, he must wear a blue shirt. So, again, for necessary assumptions search for the assumption that the argument absolutely has to have in order to make logical sense.

TIP #42: FROM NAOMI E., 176

Sometimes assumption questions will ask you to find a sufficient assumption, and then give you an answer that overdoes it. For example, all cowboys own horses; therefore, Mike the cowboy owns at least three horses. The gap here is that the evidence doesn't show that cowboys own three horses, just that they own horses, which could be only two. A correct, but tricky answer could say that the assumption was that all cowboys own no less than 10 horses.

This would make the conclusion correct; Mike the cowboy owns at least three horses since all cowboys own no less than 10 horses (so Mike owns at least three). Now this is an example of where the answer choice overdoes it. Since the answer could have been that no cowboy owns less than three horses and that would still make the conclusion follow logically, owning 10 horses just makes sure that you own more than 3. So, if you do encounter this kind of exaggerated answer, don't worry that it's not the ideal answer; if it answers the question, go with it.

TIP #43: FROM ADEN S., 177

I think the problem with assumptions is that we are so used to making them in real life without realizing it! When you walk into a restaurant, and you see a man wearing an apron and holding two plates of food on each arm, you assume he is the waiter. Even though this would probably be a good assumption, you could be wrong, and he could be bringing his own food to his family's table, wearing an apron because he doesn't want to get his clothes dirty. So you see, we are making assumptions all the time and no one is questioning them. Then comes the LSAT. Sugar is bad for your health, says the passage, so therefore soda is bad for you. In real life, you wouldn't question this type of statement, as it obviously refers to sodas with sugar. And that is why you might not catch this assumption. But on the LSAT, who said soda has sugar? Maybe it's talking about diet soda, in which case it wouldn't be bad for your health, at least according to this argument. The point is to become aware of the mental shift you need to make in order to become a better LSAT student.

TIP #44: FROM BRADLEY O., 176

Many people have problems with assumption questions. I think it is because they don't understand the definition of the word assumption. Dictionary.com has a definition that states the meaning of assumption is simply "arrogance." In other words, it's arrogant to assume. For example, someone says that Mark eats like a dog, and you assume that Mark is a person and therefore the person saying that statement said it to hurt Mark's feelings. However, the truth is that Mark *is* a dog, and so there was no intent to hurt anybody's feelings. That being said, it would be arrogant to assume that Mark is a person and then to decide that the person making the statement isn't a nice guy. This is just a way of understanding the idea of assumptions on the LSAT; basically, don't be arrogant!

TIP #45: FROM ZACK F., 175

When doing strengthening questions, don't forget that the argument is a bad one. Find the flaw in it, such as an apparent shift in scope, or whatever the flaw might be. For example, if the argument says that the amount of library books in the average library is in decline, and therefore book reading in general is in decline, the obvious shift here is from library books to books in general. That would be a flaw. To strengthen this argument, you would want to close the gap by saying that library reading is parallel to reading in general, so the decline in library reading does indicate a decline in the general population's reading. Think of a strengthener question's argument as a broken building that needs some serious repairs.

TIP #46: FROM SPENCER J., 177

You can take any given question that is in the assumption family and perform different tasks on the argument. You can try to weaken it, strengthen it or find the assumption. You can also identify the main point and possible inferences. Practicing doing different tasks all with the same question will help you understand how the same arguments can actually be used in all of the above ways and widen your understanding of the LSAT.

TIP #47: FROM PHILLIP K., 176

Strengtheners are asking you to strengthen the conclusion. This is important because when you look at the answer choices, look for an answer that has a connection to the conclusion. Furthermore, don't forget that in strengtheners, the answer often introduces completely brand new information not mentioned at all in the stimulus. This is important because it is common for people to see new information and skip over it if it looks irrelevant. Don't make this mistake because you never know what twist the answer will have!

Each of the following would strengthen the tower EXCEPT:

A. Tape
B. Glue
C. Peanut Butter
D. Band-aid
E. Chair

TIP #48: FROM GRAHAM T., 175

My tip has to do with questions that ask you to weaken the argument. First of all, these questions are similar to flaw questions. For example, the stimulus states that all books are about history. Therefore, all books are boring. An answer that would weaken that would say something like, who said that books about history are, in fact, boring? If it was a flaw question, it would say that the flaw is that the argument has taken for granted that all history books are boring. The idea here is to realize that the questions overlap and can be simply asked in different terms.

TIP #49: FROM AMANDA P., 177

A very common weakening question type has to do with cause and effect, also known as correlation vs. causation. An argument may say that A causes B. For example, when the economy is bad, businesses close. There are three ways you can disprove cause and effect. One is that it's not A that causes B, but rather it's C that causes B. So it's not the economy that causes businesses to close, but rather it's the war that is causing it. The second common answer is that A isn't causing B, but rather B is causing A. Therefore, when businesses are closing, that is creating a bad economy. The third type of answer is that A isn't causing B; there is just simply no connection between the two.

TIP #50: FROM IRIS Y., 178

If you are having problems with weakening questions, practice with the EXCEPT questions. These questions ask you to find the one answer that doesn't weaken the argument, which means that the other four answers do weaken it. Study the four wrong answers (the answers that actually do weaken the argument). This way you can see how to weaken the argument in many different ways.

TIP #51: FROM EMMA S., 180

An inference question asks you to find what is true based upon the argument above. When the question asks you what must be true, pay attention to the word "must." The common and tricky wrong answers will say something that could be true, but don't have to be true. For example, the argument says that all planes fly at a speed over 500 mph. Now what must be true? How about the fact that planes fly at 600 mph? Well, this could be true, since we know that planes fly faster than 500 mph, but they could also fly at 501 mph, and that would still be faster than 500 mph. So while the planes could fly at 600 mph, it's not a 'must,' it's a 'could.' What must be true is that planes fly faster than 499 mph, for example, or faster than 450 mph.

TIP #52: FROM ZOEY P., 175

Many times, inference questions will not contain an argument, just a set of facts. Don't let this throw you off. Since most of the logical reasoning questions are arguments, when you encounter an LR stimulus that contains no argument, just remember the facts. For example, the stronger the sun is, the faster the grass grows. The sun in country X is stronger than in the country Y. The obvious inference would be that grass grows faster in country X than in the country Y. A tricky wrong answer would be that the grass grows faster in country X than in any country in the world. Slow down here, nobody said the sun in country X is the strongest in the world, just stronger than in the country Y. Another correct answer could actually add an extra sentence. For example, the answer could say in country W, while all else is equal, the sun is weaker than in country Y, so the grass must grow slower in country W than in the country X. This is true. It just needs you to make that additional connection between the three countries.

TIP #53: FROM SCOTT E., 176

This tip has to do with inference questions. Be careful of tricky wrong answers that change the words slightly to make them look right, but they are different enough to actually be wrong! For example, the stimulus says that it is healthy to include fruits and vegetables in one's diet. The question asks you what you can infer from this. A wrong answer could say that a diet without fruits and vegetables is not healthy. Well, the stimulus didn't say that; it said that it is healthy to eat fruits and vegetables, not that a lack of fruits and vegetables is necessarily an unhealthy diet. There is a big difference. Another wrong answer would be, for example, that if one eats fruits and vegetables, he or she must be healthy. Again, the stimulus didn't say that. Don't let the LSAT trick you!

TIP #54: FROM JOEL G., 176

On inference questions, you can safely treat the entire stimulus as the premise, and the correct answer as the conclusion. Remember, they are asking you what must be true based on the above stimulus. That is exactly what a premise and conclusion are in an argument. All water is natural, unless it comes from the west. The bottle of water in front of me is not from the west. That is the premise, or in inference questions, the entire stimulus. The conclusion would be that the bottle in front of me is natural water, or on the inference question that would simply be the correct answer.

TIP #55: FROM ROSS K., 178

Main point questions are hard for many people. My tip is this: Look at the information or statement that gets backed up by some evidence. In other words, there are basically three types of functions that a sentence can have (there are, in reality, more than three, but these three are the most common). The first type, which usually comes at the beginning, is background information. For example: computers are very useful for college students. Then you have the evidence: All college students have X type of computers and Steve is a college student. Then there is the conclusion: Since Steve is a college student, so he has an X type computer. So here, the conclusion is that Steve has an X type computer. The evidence backs up this part, and here the background information just serves to get you into the conversation, so to speak. The argument would have done fine without the background information, but the LSAT wants to see if you can distinguish between what is important and what is not. Usually in main point questions the LSAT doesn't make it so clear to see. Otherwise, it wouldn't be much of a challenge. Just keep this idea in your head and look for what is being backed up with *evidence.*

TIP #56: FROM MATT L., 177

This is a great tip for students who want to improve their main point question accuracy. If you have a hard time with this type of question, go online to websites like IMDB and look up your favorite movie. Here, you will be able to view a three to four line summary of the movie. Now, to take a two-hour movie and summarize it into three lines is the holy grail of main point questions! Read a few of these summaries and you'll get a good picture of what a main point is. However, you need to make sure you read about movies that you know really well. After a few of those, try some LSAT main point questions and you should have a better idea of how to look for the main point.

TIP #57: FROM GAIL P., 179

With main point questions, you have to be careful not to mix up the main point with the conclusion. Sometimes the conclusion is the main point, but often it's not. For example, the argument may say that all nail polish is toxic. Therefore, if Molly wore nail polish, she would have something toxic on her body. So here, the conclusion of the argument is that Molly would have something toxic on her body if she was to wear nail polish, but the main point is that all nail polish is toxic. The fact that Molly would have something toxic on her body is more of an example, even if it is the conclusion here. So again, be careful not to mix up the two!

TIP #58: FROM SANDY K., 178

In the method of argument questions, you have to see what the author of the passage is trying to do. Does the author argue by analogy? Is the author using a counterexample to make her point? To become good at answering these questions, you need to be able to keep two thought processes going at the same time. One is reading what the argument is saying, and the second is thinking about how each piece ties in with each other. This skill is needed throughout your whole LSAT, and you have to decide which part of the process is more significant for the particular task you have been asked to do. For method of argument questions, the structure is more important than what exactly the argument is actually saying.

TIP #59: FROM BRANDON L., 176

My tip for method of argument questions is to practice understanding why the incorrect answers are wrong. Usually, the wrong answers will say something that the author didn't actually do. What I would recommend is simply to read the stimulus and map out what the structure of the argument is. Then look at the answer choices and compare them to the structure you've mapped out. This will really give you a sense of how to find the correct structure and, consequently, the right answers.

TIP #60: FROM JORDON H., 177

In many methods of argument questions, the stimulus contains an argument between two people; the question then asks you how the second person answers or challenges the first, or vice versa. Study these questions and see how the answers are always structural in their explaining of what the challenge was. The wrong answers can help you get familiar with the type of ways that one could respond. Not to say that the other answers are correct for the same question, but you will see how many different types of responses there are and be familiar with them.

TIP #61: FROM TYLER S., 177

This tip is for the role of statement questions. Don't focus solely on the sentence that is being referenced to in the question stem. First, read the argument and understand what the structure is. In fact, don't look at all at what the sentence is in question. Just know that the question is asking you to read for structure, not for content. Then, when you get to the question stem and find the actual sentence that is being asked about, find it and its purpose.

TIP #62: FROM RYAN H., 176

A great way I learned to practice the role of statement questions is to give your own answer before looking at the answer choices. Try to really work on understanding what the role the statement is supposed to have. By doing this, you broaden your understanding of the logical structure of the argument. It's a lot easier to see the correct answer and "feel" that it is correct, but that won't actually strengthen your logic. Again, this is only for practice – you wouldn't waste time doing this on the actual test.

TIP #63: FROM SAM K., 177

In role of statement questions, the question asks you what the role of a certain sentence was in the overall structure of the argument. Some common answers are that the role was a sub-conclusion, or that it was the general main point being proven by the argument. If you ever see an answer choice, however, that says that the role was an assumption, you know it's wrong because, by definition, an assumption is unstated. If it is stated, it cannot be an assumption!

TIP #64: FROM BEN P., 178

If you have a pretty good idea about what the role of the statement is, don't read all of the answer choices. Stop after the verbs, such as 'disproves,' 'overrides,' 'suggests,' 'helps' and 'illustrates.' If you know that the role of the statement is to disprove something, and you see an answer choice that starts with 'helps,' then you know that answer choice is wrong, so don't waste time reading it! When you do see the right verb, take the time to read the whole answer choice to make sure it is correct.

TIP #65: FROM LELA M., 177

My tip is for the parallel reasoning questions. Make sure not to get tricked with an answer choice that uses the same nouns. For example, if the stimulus is talking about dogs, the correct answer won't necessarily talk about dogs. It *could* talk about dogs, but it doesn't have to. The correct answer could talk about any other subject in the world. The key word here is structure, not content.

TIP #66: FROM BECKY P., 176

A tough part of the dreaded parallel reasoning questions is the correct answer choice could be out of order. In other words, it could have the same logical pattern, but in a different order. For example, if the argument says, "All birds fly, therefore, my bird must fly," a correct answer could say, 'My bird flies because all birds fly,' and that would be the same logic, just in a different order. Another example is if the argument says, "All tables have four legs. This thing here only has three legs, so it cannot be a table." The answer could be "because the table doesn't have four legs, it cannot be a table, for every table has four legs."

TIP #67: FROM CAMERON L., 179

Make sure you work on your time management with the parallel reasoning questions. These questions tend to have very long answer choices. I've noticed these questions can take up to twice the amount of time to get through than other questions, so if time is an issue, by all means skip these questions and come back to them. Besides being long, you need to match the answer very carefully to the stimulus, which can take time, so don't hesitate to come back to these questions at the end if needed. Eventually, if worked on enough, these questions can actually go quite fast. Before test day, assess where you are in regards to your timing of these questions and plan accordingly.

TIP #68: FROM DONNA Y., 178

My tip is about the parallel questions, but it also has to do with any question that deals with formal logic. Do your best not to diagram these questions on the actual exam. That is way too time consuming. Instead, practice diagramming these questions until you can easily do so in your head, and then you will be ready for the test.

TIP #69: FROM EDEN M., 177

My tip is about converting conditional statements. The simple equation is: if A, then B. Let's say, for example, if you are tall, then you are smart. These 'if/then' statements come up a lot on the LSAT, so make sure you know exactly how to do them! Although they can get much more complicated, I'll just explain using a simple example. The first thing to keep in mind is that 'if A, then B,' (e.g.: if you are tall, then you are smart) cannot be turned around to 'if B, then A' (e.g.: if you are smart, then you must be tall). One could be short and smart. Nor could you say 'if not A, then not B' (if you are not tall, then you are not smart). The only thing that you can infer from that equation is what's called the contrapositive. Meaning, you take the "if A, then B" equation, and you turn it around and negate it. To negate means to turn it from positive to negative, or vice versa. So now it would read 'if not B, then not A,' or in our example: if you are not smart, then you are not tall. There is no other inference that you can make from this sentence. Now please understand that this, or any other example, may very well not be the case in the real world. We all know that there is no correlation between intelligence and height. However, in the LSAT world, so to speak, "If A, then B" is a guarantee, and the contrapositive would be too.

TIP #70: FROM DANIEL T., 177

This tip is about the fallacy of an over-generalized conclusion, or when the evidence doesn't "add up" to support the conclusion. For example, if the premise says that all New Yorkers wear ties, you couldn't conclude that all Americans wear ties, or that the majority of Americans wear ties, as that would be an over-generalization. The evidence, or the premise in this case, that all New Yorkers wear ties, doesn't mean that all Americans wear ties, as we know that New York is not the majority of America. This fact that New York is not the majority of America is outside information that you would be permitted to include, as it would be considered common knowledge.[1]

---

1 See interview with Mary Adkins, page 122 JE

TIP #71: FROM RON M., 176

I want to write my tip about the fallacy called 'correlation versus causation.' Simply put, it is a logical fallacy to decide that A causes B. For example, you gave charity in the morning and then in the evening you received some great news. Is there a connection between the two? In real life, you can decide for yourself, but on the LSAT, saying that giving to charity caused the good news would be false. Could it be that there is no connection between the two? Yes. Could it be that there is a connection? Maybe, but not for sure. To conclude that there is a connection would be a fallacy.

TIP #72: FROM ELAINE O., 174

My tip is about a fallacy called "lack of evidence." Lack of evidence does not prove anything. For example, from the fact that you've never seen a pink elephant, you cannot conclude pink elephants don't exist. You can't prove something's non-existence because you have never seen it. This fallacy is quite common on the LSAT, so make sure to spot it and understand its function. I think the reason that it comes up so often is because it is an easy flaw to fall for. If a lawyer tells you that she's never seen a case where the outcome was such and such, that would sound like a good proof to most people. But now that you know about the lack of evidence fallacy, you know that while the lawyer *may* be right, she really doesn't have any *real* proof.

TIP #73: FROM JOHN O., 174

My tip is the best in this book, since out of all the tips, mine is the best. Wait a second; I think I just committed a circular logic error. That being said, let me explain this type of fallacy. When your conclusion is simply stated as the premise, as my statement was, that is called circular logic, and that is a fallacy. You can't prove

A from A. The LSAT likes to use this fallacy, maybe because it is hard to spot. The fallacy I proposed in the beginning of this tip was quite obvious, but the LSAT has a great way of hiding their flaws, so don't be fooled!

TIP #74: FROM ADAM R., 175

I want to include information in my tip about the fallacy of shifting meaning. This means that even though the meaning of a word can differ, it is a fallacy for it to shift in the middle of an argument. For example, the sentence could say "some students get kicked out of school, but this is improper, because kicking people could seriously hurt them." The word that shifted here was "kicked." The first one meant to expel a student, while the second one meant to actually kick with one's foot. When you come across these types of arguments on the LSAT, make note of the words they are using and study them.

TIP #75: FROM TOBY D., 174

Some fallacy questions on the LSAT talk about the shift in meaning of certain words in an argument. I have noticed that the arguments that do so will many times actually talk about specific words and about their meanings. This might be a good indicator that the fallacy will be in the definition of the words.

TIP #76: FROM EMILY H., 176

My tip has to do with the fallacy of logic where a bad analogy is made. For example, a bad analogy would be to say that cats and dogs are similar, as they both walk on four feet. Therefore, since cats always land on their feet, dogs always land on their feet as well. This would be treating the two groups, cats and dogs, the same because they are similar in one respect, even though they are actually quite different in other respects, and then, based off this bad analogy, coming to an erroneous conclusion. Don't fall for this fallacy. Just because the premise makes an analogy, and it makes sense at first glance, don't take it as a given; look into it carefully and see if the two subjects are in fact alike.

TIP #77: FROM CECILIA J., 178

I wanted to address a fallacy that the LSAT will try to catch you on. If you don't understand this fallacy, you might miss a few questions. If you miss a few questions, you might as well not take the LSAT. Wait, does that make sense? Sorry for scaring you, but I had to because that was exactly the fallacy I was talking about. It is called the fallacy of perfection. In other words, if something isn't perfect, that doesn't mean that it is not worth pursuing, or has no merit. So if I tell you it is not worth taking the LSAT because you might not get a 180, then that would be a logical fallacy. You could still get a great score without getting a perfect score, hence the fallacy.

TIP #78: FROM JACOB N., 177

My tip is about the fallacy called *either/or*. Meaning, that it is incorrect to assume that a certain situation has only two options, and no other. For example, if I tell you that if you are not from Florida, you must not be from America. That would be an obvious fallacy because we all know that there are forty-nine other states that one could be from and still be from the United States. However, other *either/or* fallacies are not as clear-cut. For example, a soldier tells you that if you don't enroll in the army, you are clearly not a patriot, but that is probably not true. Maybe in some people's eyes that is true, but logically speaking, one could be patriotic and not necessarily enroll in the military. When you read such a statement that has a clear *either/or* feel, consider there may be another option, because if there is in fact another option besides the two stated, the statement just committed this logical fallacy.

TIP #79: FROM BARRY G., 179

This tip is about the famous straw-man fallacy. This fallacy is committed when you focus on a certain part of an argument – usually on a minor part of it— to attack the argument as a whole. An example would be the following: psychologists say that it is healthy for children to move out of their parents' house at a certain age, as this promotes independence. However, some children, after moving out, only think about having parties, so a child moving out of his or her parents' home is not a healthy practice. You can probably sense the fallacy. Just because there may be some people who move out of their parents' houses for the wrong reason, doesn't mean that the practice as a whole is incorrect.

TIP #80: FROM ROBERT J., 175

My tip is about a common logical flaw called "reliance on an improper source." In other words, the LSAT can give you an argument that does one of two things. One flawed argument can state an opinion about something that is really a matter of fact. An example would be: "Most people believe that the average annual income in the US is $40,000. Therefore, Joe, who makes an average income, must be making $40,000." The problem is that the average income is something that can be verified; so relying on an opinion would be logically incorrect. The other flawed argument wants to rely on a professional's opinion in one discipline about a matter that concerns a different field. So if the argument tells you that the average income in the US is $40,000 because that is what Dr. Joe—who is a medical doctor—said, well that would be a fallacy. Just because the man is a medical doctor doesn't grant him expertise in economics.

TIP #81: FROM AARON C., 176

My tip is about the logical fallacy widely known as Ad Hominem. This refers to a flaw where an opinion or argument comes under attack based on an attack on the person making the argument. For example, if a doctor tells you that you need to stop smoking to recover your health, and you tell the doctor, "You have no right telling me that, since I know that you drink plenty of alcohol, and alcohol is also not healthy," that would be a classic Ad Hominem fallacy. You are attacking the person whose opinion, it is, and not addressing the real issue, which is whether smoking is or is not healthy. This fallacy comes up a lot, but even more so in my opinion, it comes up as an incorrect answer choice to an argument that doesn't actually commit that fallacy. That is why it is important to understand this fallacy, so that when the argument does not commit an Ad Hominem, you will spot it right away and move to the other answer choices.

TIP #82: FROM MICHELLE S., 179

The tip I want to share with you is about the common fallacy known as the "part to whole" fallacy. Let me give you an example. If I were to tell you that I could afford to buy any car on the car lot, I can, therefore, afford all the cars on the lot, well, that would be a logical fallacy. Just because I can afford one car, doesn't mean that I can afford all the cars. The one car is the "part" and the whole lot is the "whole." This fallacy can be presented from the opposite direction as well, i.e. whole to part. For example, if you say that since this car is heavy, each part of the car must be heavy as well, that would be wrong, because each part could be really light; but as a whole it becomes heavy. This is a common flaw and well worth remembering.

TIP #83: FROM STEVE L., 177

My tip is about the logical fallacy known as "no true Scotsman." I tell you that no Scotsman puts sugar on his porridge, and you tell me that your friend, who is Scottish, does put sugar on his porridge. Then I tell you that no *true* Scotsman puts sugar on his porridge, I will have committed this fallacy. In other words, this fallacy is about creating criteria and then not accepting anything that doesn't fall within this category. Another example is if I tell you that no New Yorker ever sleeps during the afternoon, so Michael, who is a New Yorker, either never sleeps in the afternoon, or if he does, he must not be a *true* New Yorker.

TIP #84: FROM SHOSHANNA I., 176

Let me tell you about a flaw that the LSAT tests you on, and I used to fall for it all the time. Realizing that it is a flaw helped me start noticing it. The LSAT will give you information leading to a conclusion that a certain outcome is probable, and then conclude that outcome is in fact a definite result. For example, if the stimulus tells you the only radio station Avi has ever heard play song X is the so-and-so station, therefore, since Avi is listening to song X on the radio, it must be that same so-and-so radio station. The problem being that this conclusion is not definite, even though it might be probable. If the argument says this conclusion is probable, since the evidence is probable that would be fine. The stretch from probable to definite is the issue.

TIP #85: FROM NICK K., 175

I want to tell you about a flaw that I love, because the LSAT presents it so persuasively that it's hard to catch, so please pay attention. How many people know what I am going to say? Maybe you guessed it: survey flaws. The LSAT will tell you that a survey proves something, while in many cases it doesn't. There are three reasons that a survey could be wrong. Either the survey asks the incorrect question, asks the incorrect people, or draws the wrong conclusions. We are so accustomed to accepting survey results as true that we can easily fall for a fallacious one. The LSAT will, of course, give you the facts of the survey so that you can evaluate its integrity.

TIP #86: FROM MICHAEL J., 177

My tip is about the fallacy of continuality. Many arguments mistakenly try to argue that since something has happened in the past, it will most likely continue to happen in the future. For example, the argument might tell us that since all the tests given by Professor John were multiple-choice, the next test will also be multiple-choice. While this might sound like a good argument, it is relying on time as its sole indicator. That would be the flaw of continuality.

TIP #87: FROM SARAH O., 176

A very common flaw is the flaw of percentages, and these are quite tricky, so make sure you have it down cold. 20% of LSAT students get this one wrong, whereas only 10% of GMAT students get this flaw wrong, so the total number of LSAT students who miss this flaw is greater than the total number of GMAT students who get it wrong. Is that so? Well, that was exactly the flaw. Since I didn't give you the number of students taking the LSAT or the GMAT, it would be misleading to make that conclusion. Maybe there are 10,000 LSAT students and 100,000 GMAT students, in which case 2,000 LSAT students are missing that flaw, but 20,000 GMAT students are missing it, making the argument wrong. Like I said, this is a common flaw, so make sure you understand it.

TIP #88: FROM ALEXEI T., 176

There is a logical flaw where the argument considers two groups mutually exclusive from each other. For example, if I tell you that for two hours of my day, I play chess and two hours of my day I listen to music, therefore, for four hours a day I engage in leisure time. The flaw is the two groups, i.e. the two sets of two hours each, are not necessarily *mutually exclusive*. It could very well be that I listen to music *while* I play chess. This flaw can occur while talking about two groups of people, assuming they are mutually exclusive when they aren't necessarily. 200 people in town X shop in store A, and 250 people in town X shop in store B. Therefore, you might conclude, that there are 450 people in town X altogether. But it could be that the same 200 who shop in store A also shop in store B, so maybe there really are only 250 people in town X. The reason I wrote this as my tip is because it is a flaw that is often hard to spot. After all, I told you the information in a way that sounds like they are two groups. Make sure you practice spotting this type of flaw.

TIP #89: FROM RONDA E., 178

I am here to explain my tip, which is about the flaw where two groups are compared improperly. For example, the argument tells you that the number of doctor visits in New York City annually is greater than the amount of doctor visits in Albany, New York, annually. It is therefore healthier to live in Albany than in New York City. The problem is that NYC has a higher population than Albany, so comparing the *number* of visits won't be a logical way to compare the cities' health. You would need to compare their *percentages.* If the facts are that in Albany 10% of people catch the flu every year, and in NYC 15% catch the flu, then you could say that Albany, at least in respect to the flu virus, is a healthier place to live in.

TIP #90: FROM TZVI A., 180

My tip covers a flaw where the argument assumes that two groups cannot work together. For example, the argument tells you that a college student doesn't have time to write an entire book by herself; therefore, only people who are not in college can write books. The flaw here is that it failed to consider the possibility that college students could work together. If ten college students collectively wrote a book, they would each be considered an author in their own merit, and have proven the argument incorrect. Just because they can't individually write a book doesn't mean that they can't do the job together. This is a flaw that comes up every now and then on the LSAT, so be ready for it!

TIP #91: FROM RALPH N., 174

Ignoring the consequences of actions can be considered a logical fallacy. When the argument is claiming to solve a problem without considering what side effects the solution might pose, that is a fallacy. For example, if I tell you that the best solution for our city's pollution is to get rid of the buses because they emit so much smoke into the air, what I am not considering is that the outcome of getting rid of the buses would cause more people to buy cars, which in turn would cause more pollution than the busses would. I am ignoring the consequences of my proposal, which will actually worsen the problem, and that is a flaw.

TIP #92: FROM ILYA H., 179

My tip addresses the flaw of ignoring evidence. The LSAT can say in the stimulus that a certain natural pill cures the common cold, but since most medicines are derived from chemicals and not from nature, then this pill consists mostly of chemicals, and it is well known that chemicals cannot cure the common cold. The obvious flaw here is that the argument pretends to not have heard the initial evidence, namely that the pill is *natural*, so the fact that most pills are generated from chemicals isn't relevant. Ignoring the evidence when making an argument will result in a bad argument, and hence the flaw.

TIP #93: FROM GAITRY F., 174

My tip has to do with formal logic. Formal logic is in many ways the language of the LSAT. You will need it in all three sections, maybe less so in the reading comprehension section, but you will need it for sure in the games and in the logical reasoning sections. My tip is to practice formal logic like there is no tomorrow! Write out any formal logic question that you come across. You will have to make the decision whether to write out the formal logic questions on the actual exam, but for practice purposes, write out as many of them out as you can. On the parallel logic questions, write out all the answers choices in formal logic language. This will help you to get better at formal logic, and really rock the LSAT!

Introduction to the
Logic Games Tips

T HIS SECTION IS ALL ABOUT logic games. Aren't you excited? You should be! When else will you have the incentive to perfect your spatial reasoning? Spatial reasoning has many benefits in life, but I'll let you Google those benefits when you have the time. The surest benefit, or at least the most immediate one, is that spatial reasoning can get you into law school.

When you first see the logic games they can be intimidating and a turnoff from the LSAT. Once you "get" them, however, they can be fun, challenging and growth-enhancing.

As I'm sure you've heard before, you'll never encounter a logic game in law school (unless, of course, you tutor LSAT students to make some extra cash). But the skills that you build from studying the logic games will help you in law school. If you treat the games this way – as an interesting way to prepare for law school – you might have an easier time with them.

The tips here will help you pick up on a few tricks you might not have noticed in your study guides. Study guides are dense: every page has multiple points to remember. They are not usually redundant. It's hard to remember every word on every page, but you don't need to.

That's where these tips will help. You read a tip, and ask yourself if what you just read makes sense. If it does, great. Try to use the tip and see if it's something you'd like to add to your bag of tricks. If you don't understand what it's saying, you might want to go back to your study guide or tutor and figure out if the type of game the tip is talking about is the type of game that needs more review in general.

I've always loved that the nickname for analytical reasoning is "logic games." It puts an element of fun into the equation. You have to win the game. But it's not you against the LSAT – it's you and the LSAT on the same team.

Jacob

TIP #94: FROM RAYMOND D., 175

My tip is about the logic games. Logic games can seem extremely intimidating; although the truth is that they are very learnable. I didn't believe that at first, until I saw for myself just how true that statement is. Start with studying conditional logic. You will need it on the logic games! Learn the rules and then practice them within the setting of the logic games. Learn about the general types of games. You obviously cannot learn every type at once, but start with a general knowledge of what they are. How about I list them here? The broadest way to put it, is that there are two objectives you will be dealing with. Either you need to put things in order, or you need to put things in groups. That's really it! It then breaks down into some smaller categories that all fit together. When I got this idea that there are primarily only these two objectives, the logic games became my friend.

TIP #95: FROM BELINDA D., 177

On logic games, my tip is to be careful of making unwarranted assumptions. For example, if a game says that A and B come after C and that D comes after B – you can infer that D comes after C, but you cannot infer that D comes after A. Be cautious not to make deductions that don't exist.

TIP #96: FROM CHRISTOPHER F., 175

To save time, my tip is to use the diagram you drew as your master setup for the last question in the game. After your initial setup, on the "if" questions you would usually set up another diagram. On the last question, if it is indeed an "if" question, don't waste those few seconds to set up a new one; rather, use the initial setup. I know that this tip will only save you about 20 seconds per game, but that's more than a minute on the whole section – enough time to get another question right, or to double check a previous answer.

TIP #97: FROM MICHA F., 175

I was not scoring very well at the beginning with regard to the logic game section. I was getting overwhelmed with the games, and I truly thought there was no hope! I came across this game online that I was told could help the brain with spatial reasoning; the game is called "Dual N Back." I played this game for an hour a day for two weeks. I didn't look at even one logic game during this time. When I finally did attempt a logic game after that, they simply looked so much more approachable, and the intimidation was gone! Granted, I had plenty of time before the LSAT, so I had the luxury of taking off two weeks and practicing something that is not an actual LSAT. I would advise you to employ this method only if you have ample time before the LSAT, otherwise, just focus on actual LSATs.

TIP #98: FROM SAMANTHA G., 178

With the logic games, you will see that a common question they ask is how far apart two variables can be. My tip is to try to start with the larger options. If they give you answers from six down to two, start with the six. That way, when you see that the two variables can be six spots apart, that is your answer. If six doesn't work, you move on to five, and so on. However, if you start from two and move upward, then if two works, you can't eliminate that answer until you find that three works. I think that is just too much information to keep in your head. I like to eliminate answers and cross them out in the logic games, rather than leave them as contenders, like in the logical reasoning section, for example.

TIP #99: FROM ADRIAN D., 176

Blocks are extremely helpful for the logic games. Let's say that you have six spots to fill. If you have a block of two of the variables, and in one of the questions they ask you to put the block in spots two and three, you need to ask yourself whom you can put in spot number one. Because of the other rules, you will probably only have one or two letters that can go in the first spot, and that will help you to fill in more of the diagram. Also, many times, the question will ask about a consequence that comes out of having that one variable in spot number one.

TIP #100: FROM MISHA W., 179

This tip is about loose ordering games. Let's say you have the rule that A is before B, and then you have a rule that B is before C, and then you have a rule that C is before the D. Don't create four separate rules, but rather create one long line, and in this case it would be A-B-C-D. They won't always be that simple, but even combining two or three rules can save you a lot of time on the questions. Not combining rules is the surest way to create a struggle with the logic games. Let the insurance companies be your model: combine and save.

TIP #101: FROM NEIL P., 176

On the logic games, when you find the right answer choice, fill it in and move on. Do not try to figure out if the other choices are correct. Logic games are like math. When you see a question that asks you what two plus two is and you see an answer that says four, you know that it is correct, and you wouldn't bother checking the other answers. On the logical reasoning, however, the answers are less scientific, if you will. On those, it is important to look at the other answers to see if indeed they are incorrect because there might have been a very small detail you didn't notice about the answer that you chose that made it a wrong answer. Seeing another answer that looks like it could be true will help you pick up on that.

TIP #102: FROM SALVADOR T., 175

When you start to read what a logic game is about, there tends to be a rush to quickly set up the rules in the name of saving time. The problem with this strategy is it will actually waste time! My tip, and this is something that helped me increase my logic game score by quite a bit, is to first read all the rules before diagramming *anything*. Get a sense for the game, what it's about, combine rules that connect, take a deep breath. Is there anything unique about the game? This shouldn't take more than an extra 20 seconds, but it can save you a lot more time during the game. If your initial setup is incorrect, and you have to start from scratch to set it up a second time, that can waste much more than 20 seconds. So, plan accordingly.

TIP #103: FROM RYAN D., 175

My tip has to do with the orientation questions. Sometimes you go through the rules, using each one to cross out a wrong answer. You finish this method and yet you haven't been able to cross out four answers. That's when it is time to go back to the fundamentals. For example, if the game is asking you to put six people in six different spots, if you're stuck between two answers, and you can't find a way to cross one of them out, check if one of the last two answer choices actually has all six of the people. While this is not one of the rules that you diagrammed, it is in fact a rule. Any part of the scenario, part of what the logic game says is just as important as the other rules.

Tip #104: From Adam I., 177

You will most definitely come across the following scenario. The logic game will give you a rule that says if not J, then L. The contrapositive of that would be if not L, then J. You diagram the rule. On your paper you'll see on the left side (the sufficient part) you have a not J, and the rule below that, or the contrapositive, starts with a not L; on the right side, you will have an L and below that the J, so really this is giving you three options: either you don't have J, or you don't have L, or you have them both. Make note of this in your diagram by making a spot that has these two variables with a / sign between them. This means that there will always be one of them. But don't forget that you can also have both of them. Your notation simply means that one of them is always present.

Tip #105: From Amy O., 176

Classic logic game rule, if A, then B. The contrapositive of that, if not B, then you cannot have A. So you can still have B without A. Where it gets tricky is when the rule starts with a negative. Not A, then B. Contrapositive: not B then A. So you understand that you always need one of them. What you need to remember here is that you can have both of them at the same time. What I highly recommend is to put a box around the right side of the original rule and around its contrapositive right side as well. In this case, you would put a box around the B and the A, meaning that they can go together.

TIP #106: FROM LAURA W., 177

I want to talk about must be true questions in the logic games section. A must be true question is basically an inference that you have to make. Sometimes you made the inference and jotted it down, and sometimes you did not see it. If you did not see the inference, don't worry; it might not be something that affects all the other questions, especially when the answers are vague. For example, if the rules say that A is before B and B is before C in a strict sequencing game, and then you have a must be true question that says, "The earliest C can be is 3," those types of inferences are not something you would diagram. It should be simple enough to see, even though the LSAT can and does ask such simple questions. On the other hand, after you answer the must be true question and come up with a concrete answer, make sure to note that in your main diagram.

TIP #107: FROM JUDAH K., 174

In must be true questions, a lot of times answers will be hard to spot. However, what will be easy to spot are incorrect answers. My tip is to not be arrogant. You don't have to find the correct answer all the time. Sometimes you have to look for easy cross outs and work the process of elimination. This may sound like a simple idea, but in reality, if you have long answer choices in a must be true question, it can save you a lot of time by looking for the wrong answers and crossing them out.

TIP #108: FROM ANDREW Y., 175

My tip might be different from other tips in this book because I'm not talking about a technique or specific method. Rather, I'm talking about what your mindset should be when you approach logic games. A major problem with logic games is that we attempt to do too many games without learning how to approach them. This causes people to believe that the logic games are incredibly hard, and that can cause resentment towards the games. Try to forget about your first impression of the games and start to like or even love the logic games. You might ask, what is there to love about games? Well, for one, they'll get you into law school. Now, once you're in law school you might be surprised that you'll never, ever have to do a logic game. However, the *skills* that you have acquired while studying for logic games are extremely applicable. So, in a sense, studying for the logic games is actually preparing you for law school. And that is a good reason to love the logic games.

TIP #109: FROM ASHLEE S., 178

The number-one skill you need for logic games is short-term memory. Even though you diagram all the rules of each logic game, if you don't commit the rules to short-term memory, it will be hard to follow and complete logic games without any mistakes. The main rules you need to remember throughout the game are the rules that play a major part in most of the game. For example, rules such as not having two consecutive variables. If we can't have two J's or two L's or two N's together, that is probably an important rule that will play throughout the entire game, and this is something you want to commit to short-term memory.

TIP #110: FROM VICKY J., 175

I discovered the following strategy, and I offer it as my tip. It's based off strengthening exercises that are done throughout many sports. As an illustration, in soccer, the goalie stands at the goal while dozens of soccer balls are being kicked at him or her. Then, during a real game, the goalie will only deal with one ball. Practicing guarding the goal against dozens of balls at once makes one ball seem simple. How could one use this idea to practice for the LSAT? This is the idea I came up with, and it works pretty well. After practicing a logic game, and after not seeing that game for a day or two, do the entire game without using a pencil. Diagram nothing! Use only your head! After doing a few games just in your head, using a pencil and paper will make it seem so easy, and you won't understand when someone tells you that the logic games are hard!

TIP #111: FROM DAVID Z., 174

In the logic games, especially in sequencing games, you are always looking to create limited options. Limited options mean creating at least two or sometimes three or four principal diagrams. These principal diagrams should consist of most of the different scenarios that you might come across and will make solving the logic game easier. The question is off of which rule should you make the limited options? In other words, let's say that you have a game with the following rules: S is either one or six, and R is either second or third. So off which rule should you generate your limited options? The answer is, and here is my tip, you want to build your limited options based off the rule that takes up the most space. So in the example before, S can be first or six and R can be second or third, look at the other rules and see if any of them combine with one of these rules. The next rule is that S has to have L next to it. So making limited options with the S rule means taking up more room.

TIP #112: FROM BRIAN N., 176

In sequencing games, there is one common mistake that people make, and I would like to address this slip-up in my tip. When it says A is two spots *before* B, then if A is first, B is third. However, when it says that there are two spots *between* A and B, that would be a *completely* different story. If A is first, then B is fourth. Many games use these rules, and if you don't have them down cold you're going to get confused. Because this is such a simple mistake to make, the LSAT counts on you to do so and will ask a question or two that will test your understanding of this rule.

TIP #113: FROM SHARON S., 177

My tip is about the sequencing logic games. An important distinction I was working on was to remember that there are games where you have a one-to-one ratio, or a seven-to-seven ratio. In other words, there are seven spots that need to be filled with seven variables, which is the simple version of sequencing games. But you can also have seven spots with eight variables, or with five variables, in which case the variables go either more than once, or a spot is filled with more than one variable at the same time, or not all the variables have to go. And then of course you have some sort of brand new game on test day, like I had. The point is to be flexible with your approach to games; just because you see a word like "consecutive," which usually means that the game is a sequencing game, don't forget that there can be many differences between games.

TIP #114: FROM NINA M., 175

I always had major problems with multiple layered sequencing games, where you have to match variables to spots, such as O through U to 1 through 7, and then also match qualifiers, such as doctor or nurse to the O through U. I found the best way to do these games, as far as the setup goes, is to have two lines, one line for the O-U and one line for the D for doctor and N for nurse. Furthermore, in the name of simplifying the game and making it more visual, I write the O-U next to the line where they go, and the letters D and N next to their line. This way, I always remember what needs to go where. I think that this tip can help you to organize these types of games.

TIP #115: FROM DELILAH C., 174

My tip has to do with the sequencing type of logic games. These tend to be the easiest of the games. From the experience I gained going over most of the LSATs, I've noticed that *usually* these are the first games of the section, although not always. The reason I believe that these games are quite simple, is they are very similar to each other, so once you *master* a few dozen of them, there is not much that the LSAT can throw at you to confuse you. My tip, therefore, is to make sure you get really good at them, because that will give you more time for the harder games.

TIP #116: FROM JUSTIN E., 175

My tip has to do with diagramming deductions. Most test prep companies teach you to diagram in the following way: if A has to go before B (in a sequencing game), then you need to write a sign such as A-B to indicate that, which is perfectly fine. My problem is when they teach that you then proceed and make a deduction that if A is before B, then that means that A cannot go last, and that B cannot go first. Well, duh! Don't waste your time making these elementary deductions! Maybe at the very beginning of your studying you should make these deductions, but if you are shooting for a top score, don't bother. Your time would be much better spent trying some hypothetical setups, or virtually anything else. The point is to be a smart test taker and use your time wisely.

TIP #117: FROM MIA K., 176

I wanted to make a point about the games. In the name of getting more questions right, some students will skip games that look more complicated, in order to focus on the other three games. The thought is to not waste time on one game, which might cause you to only complete two games out of the four. Instead, this school of thought dictates, complete three out of the four, leaving the hardest game to the end. And while that is a legitimate strategy, my tip is not to get intimidated by the *size* of the game, as some of the longer games can be easier than the shorter ones. If there are specific games that cause you the most trouble, by all means leave it for the end, but don't choose which games to skip based on the *length* alone.

TIP #118: FROM MEGHAN L., 174

My tip might sound like an obvious one, but it's really not that obvious to many people. My tip is: on the logic games, write clearly! Under the timed pressure, it is too easy to misread a dash, such as L-M, meaning L is before M, as an arrow, which would mean if L, then M. I made a lot of those mistakes, and it can be really annoying to miss a question because you can't read your own handwriting. So I guess my tip is for those who should be a doctor based on their handwriting, if you want to be a lawyer, you have to write clearly on the logic games and on the answer sheet!

TIP #119: FROM AUSTIN C., 174

My tip is to pay attention to a rule that says two variables are consecutive. If it says R and M are consecutive, please don't misread that to say that R is before M! That is a very painful error to make, because that will cause a lot of mistakes on that game. The reason that it is so easy to fall for that is because the rule introduces one before the other, as there is no other way, of course. But I think that is evident from the fact that while students do make the mistake that R is before M, you won't see anybody misinterpret that rule to say that M is before R. Being aware of this common mistake will help you avoid it.

TIP #120: FROM EUGENE R., 179

My tip has to do with sequencing games that have a vertical setup rather than the more common horizontal setup. My method is to do all games in the traditional horizontal diagram. The reason for this is consistency. In other words, since most games are horizontal, it can be quite confusing when you come across a vertical one, so I say *bend the game to you!* If before and after is left and right respectively, then up is right and down is left. Just think of it as the order of letters, so if A is higher than B, that would mean that A is more to the right than B. It's really not hard to adapt the game to the horizontal setup, and it will be less confusing for you.

TIP #121: FROM JAY T., 174

Let's say you have a diagram with spots 1-7, with M on spot 4. Then you have a rule that A, B, and C are after M. So now you know that A, B, and C are in spots 5, 6, and 7, although not necessarily in that order. My tip would be to now write the letter A, B, and C above the spots 5, 6, and 7, but make sure to notate with commas that indicate they don't have to be in that order. This is trickier when you have another rule that puts A before B. Now you know that either A is in 5 or 6, and B is in either 6 or 7, and that C can be in any of the three spots. Here too, make sure that you notate and understand your notation to mean that A is before B, but that C can be before, after or in between the two. I would mark A-B and C above them. It works quite well when you are in a rush to answer questions, and you don't have time to go back and look at the rules to double check.

TIP #122: FROM MIRIAM A., 179

My tip is to think literal. I walked into the post office today with a package that was destined to an international address. There were two slots that I could put the package into. One said, "Local mail only" and the other one said, "All other mail." I asked the clerk if I could put international mail into the "All other mail" slot. He said, "all" means "all," no?

TIP #123: FROM SAMMY K., 176

My tip is about grouping games. What is very important to notice is if there are supposed to be a certain amount of people, birds, clowns or whatever in each group. It is easy to assume that if we have six students and two teachers that each teacher has three students, but that does not have to be the case! Read the scenario carefully to make sure you understand what you are dealing with.

TIP #124: FROM JACK M., 174

I wanted to talk about games that ask you to split a group of letters into two groups. My tip is to always make sure you know if all the letters need to be assigned to a group, or if it is okay to have a letter live in limbo land. Just because the game wants us to make groups, doesn't mean all the letters have to be used.

TIP #125: FROM LYNN H., 178

In the in-and-out games, I found the following two types: both have you put some variable in and the others out, but one type will have a specific number of variables that are in and out, and the other type will not have that rule restriction. In the scenario that gives you a specific number of ins and outs, make lines that represent the amount of variables that are in and the amount that are out.

TIP #126: FROM JORDAN P., 174

My tip is about splitting games, i.e. grouping games that have two groups. Pay attention to whether or not all the variables need to be used. If they do all need to be used, you will probably have rules that tell you that two variables, such as J and K, cannot go together. In this case, like the name of the game suggests, make a split and put a J/K on each side, as we know that they both need to be used but can't go together. This basically fills up a full spot on each side, making the game much easier.

TIP #127: FROM MADISON N., 178

My tip is about conditional rules of logic games. This might be a straightforward tip, but it is worth reiterating. Whenever you have a conditional rule, always diagram the rule and its contrapositive. The contrapositive is just as important as the original rule, as it is exactly the same in essence. But instead of you having to reverse and negate in your head every time, you already have it diagrammed on your paper, and this saves a lot of much needed time.

TIP #128: FROM BELLA I., 174

"If and only if…" That is a fun rule to have. G goes, if, and only if, R goes. Or, if you have a G, then, and only then, will you have

R. Either way, what the rule is telling you is that G only goes if you have an R, and R only goes if you have a G. As far as diagramming it, you need a double arrow, with G and R on one side each. But don't forget that the contrapositive will also have a double arrow, so if G doesn't go, then neither does R, and vice versa. This is one of the few concepts you need to actually memorize on the LSAT.

TIP #129: FROM BRODY O., 178

My tip is to make sure you understand how to translate "and" and "or" into their appropriate contrapositives. The contrapositive of "and" is "or," and the contrapositive of "or" is "and." So, if A and B attend the party, then so does C; the *contrapositive* would be that if C doesn't attend, then A or B don't attend. If L or M attend, then so does J, so if J doesn't attend, then both L and M don't attend.

TIP #130: FROM CHRISTINA C., 178

On grouping games you might come across the following scenario: You have three groups, each with exactly two spots. Then you have a rule that H is always with G. Should you create three separate diagrams, with H and G filling up one of the groups in each setup? The answer is that it depends. If that will have consequences in the other groups and thereby narrow down the game, it is probably worth it. If, however, the groups don't have any significance as far as what number group they are in, it probably won't help much. What I want you to take away from my tip is that creating a few options can be helpful in the right case, but use your judgment as to whether it is worth the time.

TIP #131: FROM TAYLOR S., 179

For in and out games, pay close attention to rules that require one or another letter to always be in. You have this in a case in which it says that if the blue team is out, then the red team is in. So, if the red team is out, then the blue team is in. Either way, at least one of them will be in, so make a spot for this, and mark it blue/red. That way, one spot is already taken, and you have made the game one spot smaller. But also don't forget that they both could be in at the same time, although they both can't be out.

TIP #132: FROM LEON B., 176

In splitting grouping games, where you have two groups to be filled with all the variables, you will find this tip helpful. The rule states that if M is in group 1, then P is in group 2. So the contrapositive would be if P is not in group 2, then M is not in group 1. But since there are only two groups, it would make much more sense to diagram the contrapositive this way: if P is in group 1 (which is forced from the fact that P is *not in 2*), then M is in 2. If you have three groups, this won't help, because if P is not in 2, P could be either in 1 or 3, but with two groups, this can save you a lot of time.

TIP #133: FROM CLAIRE E., 177

Many grouping games contain sub-groups. For example, there could be cats, A, B, C and D, and dogs, E, F, G and H. If you have clear handwriting, you might want to consider writing the cats in uppercase letters, and the dogs in lowercase letters. If your handwriting isn't incredibly neat, forget it! It will just mix you up, especially with letters like K or C, in which the lowercase and uppercase letters are the same shape with only a difference in size.

TIP #134: FROM KYLIE T., 176

My tip is about grouping games with sub-groups. What can be confusing is when some of the letters are in both groups. Usually there are two neat groups with, let's say, four letters in each. But then you come across a game with two groups and letters that overlap. This can be extremely confusing, so I would recommend first of all remembering that letters could overlap, then recognizing if they do, and if in fact they do, circling those letters that overlap between the two or three groups. While this method may take a few extra hundredths of a second, it can save you time by ensuring that you won't get confused with the sub-groups.

Introduction to the Reading Comprehension Tips

T HIS NEXT PART IS ALL about the reading comprehension section. When I was collecting these tips I asked the students why they picked a certain section or idea as their tip. The common theme was their love for that particular section. You may ask yourself, "How can I love reading comprehension?"

As Herman Wouk writes in his book, *City Boy,* through the words of Herbie Bookbinder, "Everything is perspective." If you see the LSAT in general or the reading comprehension in particular, as evil, it'll be hard to love it. Many (probably most) high scorers regard the LSAT in the same way they would a ruthless gym coach. It pushes you, it trains you and it shoves the truth in your face. You get out of line? It straightens you out. You give up on it? It doesn't come running after you. You want to get back inside? It doesn't resist.

If you view the LSAT like that – as a free brain, logic or endurance trainer – love of the LSAT is not only an option – it's inevitable.

You will notice the tips in this section vary greatly. Some may even seem contradictory. That is because each person learns differently. You should not be encouraged to use one, and only one, technique just because it worked for someone else.

When I was younger, I took voice lessons. Over six years, I went to seven different voice teachers. Each had his or her distinctly different methods. Most of them not only told me that their methods were the best, but that any other method would only damage my voice. And yet there was one teacher who understood that each person learns differently, and should be taught with this in mind. That's the teacher I stuck with. Some methods work for some people, while same methods may wreak havoc on others. The key is to have an open mind and learn what works for you.

The LSAT and methods for its mastery are no different. Try out various methods, and find the one that works best for you. Experiment! Have fun! Eventually you'll realize that reading comprehension isn't all that bad, *and learn to love it!*

Jacob

TIP #135: FROM AVERY E., 180

My tip is about a new way to approach the reading comprehension section. So, this is the thing: We learn by association. When great speakers are on a stage, they will sometimes use the association technique. When they are talking about a bad thing, something unwanted, something to avoid, or something evil, they will go to the right side of the stage, or raise their volume, or raise their right hand only. Then, when they address the opposite – the thing that you want, something good – they will go to the left side of the stage, or lower their volume, or raise their left hand only. When reading the passages, when you come across the main point, point to it with your index finger, for example. When you read opinion number one, use the lead side of your pencil to point at it, and the eraser to point to side number two. These are all just examples; find methods that make sense to you, but just make sure to stay consistent with them. You can also hear in your head the sound of trumpets sounding as if they are accepting the new king into his kingdom when you find the main point, or a Mickey Mouse voice saying the old methods or thoughts or theories that the passage is about to refute, and offer new and promising evidence against.

TIP #136: FROM JOSH G., 174

This one tip was responsible for an increase of over five points on my reading comprehension section. While reading the passage, focus on the issues, also known as the arguments. The rest of the text is just examples, which are not nearly as important as the arguments as far as the comprehension of the passage goes. The questions will also ask about the examples given, but for those questions, you can always simply look back at the passage. Focus on the arguments and how each paragraph ties in with the other. This is the *real essence* of understanding the reading comprehension passages.

TIP #137: FROM LUCAS B., 174

When you review the reading comprehension questions, make sure you understand exactly which words in the passage answer each question, and underline them. The trick to reading comprehension is understanding how you can infer, from just a few words, the author's tone, intention, and many other things. This nitty-gritty type of studying the RC section will not only make you much better at the section, but will also improve your reading and inference-making skills, which is vital in law school.

TIP #138: FROM LINDA V., 176

My tip is about the reading comprehension section. For me, the best method is to simply summarize each paragraph in a short sentence. When I finish the whole passage, I look at the summaries, and then jump into the questions. The details can always be double-checked if needed. However, the main point of each paragraph and the passage as a whole is something you should commit to memory and don't have to look back for.

TIP #139: FROM GLORIA L., 177

My tip is actually about something that you shouldn't do, and that is looking at the questions on the reading comprehension section before you read the actual passage. Although this is a highly popular method with the logical reasoning, with the reading comprehension, it will only cause you confusion. The logical reasoning passages are short, so it is not hard to remember your job, so to speak, whether it is to find an assumption or to weaken an argument. The reading comprehension passages, however, are long, dense, and convey a lot of information. Trying to keep the questions in your head while reading all that would not be wise. It will simply cloud your comprehension.

TIP #140: FROM MARINA M., 176

When practicing the reading comprehension, really study the question types. There are only about six main types, and knowing exactly what they are, will give you a much better perspective when you are reading the passages. Think of it like this (example by analogy?), if you have a reading assignment, and you will be asked about the names of places that are visited in the reading material, when you read you will be focused on the names of the places and not so much on the actual story or the people. Since you know ahead of time what the questions will be, you will know what to focus on.[2]

TIP #141: FROM SASHA D., 176

While speed-reading is not recommended for the reading comprehension, there are a few tricks that they teach in speed-reading which can be beneficial. For example, one is reading a few words at a time. Let's say you are driving to New York, and you see a sign that says, "New York City." You might notice the word "City," but the two words "New York" just seem as if they go together, even though, in reality, they are two separate words. Practice reading a few words at a time, this will speed up your reading, and also improve your comprehension. Imagine if you had to think about the word "New" and then separately the word "York." You would be thinking about a new York, how new is it? Is there an old York? That would be annoying. Instead, "New York" just comes off as it is, without much thinking. This tip can speed up your reading by about 30%.

TIP #142: FROM KARINA A., 177

On the reading comprehension section, and it is important to notice and understand certain words and know their role. Words such as "however," "in contrast," and "some argue" are words that

---

2 This does not contradict the previous tip. Tip #139 was to about not reading the actual questions on each passage. This tip is advising that you know what the questions are in general, so you will notice certain ideas in the passage, such as main point, tone etc. JE

indicate a change in the flow of the passage. In other words, if until now the passage makes a certain claim, then uses words like "however," you would be correct in assuming the passage now is taking a different direction. Spotting these words will help you to understand not just what the sentence says, but how it functions in the passage as a whole.

TIP #143: FROM MAX S., 174

I want to bring up the technique of underlining certain words or sentences in the passage. This is a subject that some experts will swear by, while others would argue it just wastes time. My take is somewhat a combination of the two. The act of underlining does help your focus, and if done right, helps you to focus on the right parts of the passage. On the other side, underlining also slows you down, and as we all know, on the LSAT time is pressing. That's why I advocate an approach that combines the two schools of thought. Start off by practicing untimed reading passages and underline key words or phrases. After going over the passage at least twice, check to see if what you underlined truly was the essence of the passage. Next, do the questions, really focusing on if what you underlined was relevant to answering the questions. After doing around twenty passages using that method, start to read passages and underline *in your head.* By now, you would have picked up on what is truly essential to underline, and be able to make a mental note of those sentences.

TIP #144: FROM SHIRA J., 174

My tip has to do with your state of mind while reading a reading comprehension passage. Take into consideration the feel of the passage. For example, is the author excited and full of energy? Or is the passage dry and chock-full of facts? The subject, but mainly the tone of the passage, can draw you into its energy. I've noticed the more exciting the passage is, the easier it is to read, and consequently, easier to answer the questions. You might be wondering how this helps you since you cannot choose which passages to get put into your exam, but my tip here is for you to *pay attention to the mindset the passage puts you in.* If you notice you are being drawn into that boring mindset, well, sit up! Shake your knees and energize yourself. The idea is that it is important to notice if you are all of a sudden not so alert, as certain passages can cause you to be, and plan a strategy ahead of time.

TIP #145: FROM PARKER S., 175

I suggest you practice reading magazines to improve your reading skills. Reading magazines such as the *Economist* helps you in two ways. One, it gets you into the groove of reading. The more you read, the better, and reading non-LSAT material will help you make that transition without wasting valuable real LSATs. The second benefit is that a magazine like the *Economist* has articles about a wide range of subjects. The LSAT has passages about every subject known to man, and sometimes the subject itself can throw you off. In an attempt to broaden your comfort level, read articles on topics you wouldn't normally read.

TIP #146: FROM KELLY W., 176

My tip has to do with focus, and although focus is an important skill needed for the whole test, my tip is specifically for the reading comprehension section. What's interesting about focus is that we are *always* focusing. The question is what are we focusing on? When you read a long passage, there are so many places for your mind to wander. If you start reading about a certain subject, let's say about mayors of major cities, it might remind you about the time you interned for the mayor of your town and the time you met with her. You *are* focusing, just not on the right mayor! I believe the real question you need to ask yourself isn't, "How do I focus?" but rather ask yourself, "How do I *shift* my focus?"

TIP #147: FROM MOLLY G., 177

Be careful of getting too comfortable with any specific reading comprehension passages' style. For example, most passages have two or three opposing opinions or arguments. If the question was what came first, the chicken or the egg, then the side that says that the egg came first is in disagreement with the opinion that says the chicken came first. You might get comfortable with that type of passage, but then comes along a passage with two opinions that are not opposing. For example, the passage could talk about why entrepreneurs start businesses. One opinion states that entrepreneurs start businesses because they are looking for financial freedom, while the other opinion states that entrepreneurs don't like working for other people, and that's why they start businesses. If not outright stated, these two opinions are not disagreeing. Each side could agree with the other one. Even though you have two opinions, you don't have a dichotomy. So again, don't get too used to any specific passage structure, as they can change.

TIP #148: FROM KENNETH T., 178

When practicing reading comprehension, be aware that while most passages contain some sort of argument, there are also fact-based passages. While most passages are in the first person, some are in the third person. You never know what the LSAT will throw at you, so my tip is to be flexible. Also, try reading tough reading material outside the LSAT, such as various law schools' law reviews. By strengthening your general reading skills you will be more prepared if you are served a curve ball on test day.

TIP #149: FROM LAWRENCE O., 175

Pay close attention to the author's opinion. In many reading comprehension passages, the author explains a two-sided argument, and then tells you what he or she thinks. The author might be siding with one side of the argument, or the author might have his or her own opinion. This is important. When you are practicing, read slowly, and really try to see the difference between what the author states as opinions of the argument, and what the author's own opinion is. The author may also have an opinion about one of the views, meaning that the author can refute or challenge one of the sides taken. While the actual argument seems to be the main idea, it is really the author's take on the argument that we are concerned with.

TIP #150: FROM JONATHAN R., 174

In the reading comprehension section, beware of answer choices that are out of scope. For example, if the passage says that most diamonds are clear, meaning they have no color, you cannot infer that most jewelry has a clear color, since we don't know what percentage of jewelry is diamonds. An answer like this might seem correct, because it has the same key words, but it is out of scope.

TIP #151: FROM NASIR S., 176

My tip is a bit interesting, as it has to do with the future of the LSAT. When the LSAT introduced comparative reading in June of 2007, students became alarmed as to the LSAT's future. What would happen if one studies for the LSAT using the old exams, and then on test day there is a brand-new format? Well, three things. One, LSAC, the council that writes the LSATs, writes in their own books about strategies and ways of approaching the LSAT. So it would be safe to assume that if they were to make any major changes, they would notify us, as well as take their books of their website. Second, the comparative reading, while being new, isn't that much different that it would blow somebody completely away if they saw it for the first time. Changes like that shouldn't knock you off your feet, because if they do, you will be in for a big surprise in law school.[3] And third, even when there have been changes, they have all been one at a time. I highly doubt that the LSAC will all of a sudden change the entire test completely. Besides, from my knowledge, the law schools are quite happy with the LSAT, so there doesn't seem to be any need for change.

TIP #152: FROM CODY H., 178

The comparative passages can be quite simple if you know what to look for. Simply put, they usually talk about the same issue. Once you understand what the main theme is, just note to yourself what each passage says. Then pay attention to see if the passages work with or against each other. I would advise using notation, even though I wouldn't usually do so on the other passages, because it can be hard to remember which passage said what.

---

3 The other changes that the LSAT instituted, such as the two page layout for the logic games and the equivalent rule, also on the logic games, were all introduced on June exams. JE

TIP #153: FROM SEAN T., 176

Comparative passages always took me much longer than the regular passages. That's why I would recommend leaving it for last, if you also feel that it takes you longer. If you leave it for last, you will see exactly how much time you have, and it won't steal time from the other passages. All questions are worth the same amount of points; there is no extra credit for the harder questions, so plan accordingly.

TIP #154: FROM WESTON S., 177

This tip is about the main point questions in the reading comprehension section. How do you find them? Simply find the central theme, add that to the conclusion of the entire argument, and voila, you have your main point. I know it sounds simple, but it works. You will see that the four wrong answers on the main point questions have to do with the central theme, but neglect to point out the conclusion. Maybe even one or two answers will not talk about the central theme at all, so that makes them easy cross outs. Find the conclusion, many times at the end of the whole passage (but not necessarily), and simply add the actual words of the central point of the passage.

TIP #155: FROM TAMMY P., 176

My tip might scare you, as it has to do with the science passages. Science passages are a drag for a lot of students, for the LSAT is for prospective law students, and prospective law students are not usually interested in science to begin with. Don't worry; there's hope. Start by reading some science books. Watch some science videos on YouTube, especially about types of science you are not as familiar with. Just make science your friend, and don't hesitate when you come across a science passage. They can actually be easier than non-science passages; the only difference is when you see a law-related passage you might get excited that you are finally reading something that has to do with the law, and when you see science, you pause for a moment, dreading the next few minutes. So make science fun, and at least *pretend* to like it.

TIP #156: FROM JACOB L., 176

When reading science RC passages, the tendency is to read with an eye on the details. The fact that you might not understand science as well as other subjects might cause you to try to read the passage slower or to summarize more or take more notes. This is a mistake. Read with the identical depth you would read any other passage, focusing on the structure and the arguments the same as you would with other passages. When it comes to the actual subjects, you will always have the subject, let's call it "A," and usually two sides to an argument, "B" and "C." Now the A, B, and C will be different in every passage, but the relation between the A, B and C won't. So whether the A, B, and C are atoms, molecules or quirks, just think of them as the A, the B, and the C.

TIP #157: FROM WARREN B., 175

My tip has to do with using the structure of reading comprehension passages as a tool to understand the passage. Think of it like this: Why did the author stop the paragraph in a certain place? It's because a point was made. When a seasoned trial lawyer is questioning a witness on the stand, once the witness said what the lawyer wants to hear, the lawyer says, "No more questions." Any further questions would just cloud up the actual message the lawyer wants the jury to hear. The same goes for the reading comprehension passages. Once the author made the point, he or she continues to the next paragraph. Ask yourself, at the end of each paragraph, what did the author tell me in this paragraph and why did they stop the paragraph at this exact point?

TIP #158: FROM WILLIAM J., 175

My tip has to do with improving your reading comprehension, given that you have some time before the actual exam. This happened to me nearly by chance while I was studying for the LSAT. Even though I was almost graduating, I realized that I had a writing class requirement I needed to fulfill in order to complete my degree. I took the CLEP exam for college writing, and I found that working on my writing actually also helped me a lot with my reading! Just understanding how certain things work in English gave me quite a boost. Even if you don't have an English class right now, try brushing up on your writing skills, it can do wonders for your reading abilities.

TIP #159: FROM OLIVIA F., 177

On the comparative passages, there is often a question that asks about the relationship between the passages. These questions can be difficult because you have to compare the passages as a whole and also compare the two words in the answer choices. For example, an answer choice might be that the relationship of the two passages is like a tennis racket to a tennis ball. But what is that exact relationship anyway? I actually found these questions to be quite mentally stimulating during the practice. I suggest putting in a little bit of extra time during practice to dissect these questions and answers because it can help you develop comprehension.

TIP #160: FROM LORRAINE S., 177

The tip I want to give you here improved my reading comprehension section by a few points. The tip is simple yet profound. What I was doing, in the name of saving time, was reading the passage and starting the questions right away. The fact that I always finished the section with a few minutes to spare didn't help, as the amount of correct answers was not that high. Then I discovered this simple tip, which is to take a breath after reading the passage. Let the data sink in. As you take the breath, think about the main points of each paragraph and literally give yourself ten seconds just to absorb everything. You will be astonished at how much this can help you.

TIP #161: FROM VIVIAN C., 176

When a question asks you about a specific line in the passage, always read a line or two (or even three) before the line that is referenced in the question. This will give you the context of the line, not just the actual sentence. Furthermore, read at least one sentence after the referenced line. Again, this will give you the context within the sentence, which makes a huge difference in comprehension. Also, when you look at a certain sentence, take note of whether in that paragraph there is any argument or basic information crucial to the whole passage.

TIP #162: FROM ALBERTO A., 175

I was getting two or three questions correct on each reading comprehension passage until I discovered this tip. It may seem obvious, but to me, it wasn't! I was reading the passage, with a basic understanding of it, and then jumping straight into the questions. I started to spend much more time on the passage, and consequently, less time struggling with the questions. I was doing the exact opposite: reading the passage in the "suggested" three and a half minutes, and spending the rest of the time on the questions. Once I switched priorities, my score went up to almost 100%. This may or may not also help you. You might be spending too much time on the passage, so don't take this tip blindly. But if you do find yourself finishing the passage and then struggling with the questions, this tip might help you.

TIP #163: FROM WHITNEY K., 179

I found this tip when I was studying and having some difficulties in the RC section. I was having enough trouble with the law and history-related passages, but with the science passages – forget it! I simply could not wrap my head around them. The tip I discovered helped me tremendously, and here it is. Take a hard passage; it doesn't have to be a science passage, just any hard passage. Read it again and again and really take in all the details, names, opinions and examples. Remember, this is just for this specific exercise; this wouldn't be the way you read during the exam or even during practice exams. Now, find a friend who is willing to take the time, and relate all of the information to him or her. Engage in a discussion about the passage's topic. *This takes your comprehension to the next level*. It's one thing to read a passage and get some multiple-choice questions right; it's a whole other thing to be able to have a conversation about a dense topic, while recalling every detail, and putting up your own arguments.

TIP #164: FROM FRANCISCO J., 175

My tip is about your focus during the reading comprehension passages. Besides the main point and the arguments or issues in the passage, there will be a lot of details and examples. It can be too easy to concentrate on the examples and details (wrong) and not on the main point or thesis (right). My advice is this: keep going back in your mind and evaluate how what you are reading is *connected with the thesis*. This idea carries over to the questions as well. Unless asked about a very specific detail, keep in mind that the correct answer should relate to the main idea or point of the passage.

TIP #165: FROM MICHAEL H., 177

I thought of this idea when I was studying for the LSAT. I was having trouble with recalling the details or where in the reading comprehension passage something was stated. This tip won't help you if you have a few weeks before the exam, but if you have a few months, this tip can help a great deal. What I started to do was to notice, for example, a name of a restaurant that I saw driving home, and also notice the address. When I got home, I would try to recall the exact name and address. I would look at the license plates on random cars and try to remember the number, without putting in too much effort. The point is to use these small opportunities during the day to strengthen your short-term memory, and it can work wonders.

TIP #166: FROM KELLY W., 176

I found that the most important sentence, and the hardest one to understand in the RC passages, is the *first sentence*. The reason it might be hard is because people tend to get nervous at the beginning. Once you get through a few sentences, you forget about the LSAT and actually start to focus on the subject. The problem is that starting to focus only after a few sentences can be quite detrimental to the comprehension. My advice here is to *read the first sentence twice*. Let the initial time be with the pressure, the second time for comprehension. Of course, if you can already concentrate well from the first read, don't bother with it a second time, but if you find yourself not focused during the first time, by all means read the first sentence again. The reason why the first sentence is often so important is that it includes the main point of the whole passage, so even if your focus was good during the first read, you will probably benefit from a second read anyway.

TIP #167: FROM STEVE T., 175

If you have some time before the LSAT, practice your vocabulary. My vocabulary wasn't great, and it proved to be quite a challenge. Many questions were determined by the meaning of one word. There are lists on the Internet that detail the main words the LSAT likes to use. You could simply keep a list for yourself when going through the logical reasoning or reading comprehension, and make sure you study them. The absolute best way to practice vocabulary is not to study and repeat the lists, but rather to use the words in everyday conversation. Simply pick a few words a day that you want to remember, learn their meaning, and make a point throughout the day to use those words while talking to others. For example, I wanted to remember the word 'smug,' which means 'self-satisfied.' I came home to my apartment and saw my roommate. I told him, "Why, you sure do look smug!" He of course had no idea what I meant, so he had to look it up as well, and then got mad at me for not wanting to explain to him the meaning of it. Boy, have I remembered that word ever since!

TIP #168: FROM CAROL R., 176

This tip helped me almost instantly with reading comprehension. I actually heard about it in a speed-reading course, and although speed-reading is not a smart technique for the LSAT, this aspect of it helped me tremendously. The idea is simple, and I've tried it with dozens of reading comprehension passages, so I know it works across the board. What you've got to do first, read the first sentence of every paragraph. Then read the entire passage. The first sentence normally sums up the whole paragraph, so it really gives you a good sense of where the passage is going. I highly recommend this method, as it helped me go from 18 out of 28 to 26 out of 28. I think the numbers speak for themselves.

TIP #169: FROM MICHAEL J., 175

I want to talk about a very helpful approach to reading comprehension for the LSAT. The idea is the LSAT has its own language. In other words, in everyday language we can switch one word for another. For example, if someone tells you that you have a lot of life experience, and you interpret that to mean that you're smart, and that would be okay. But not in LSAT land. The LSAT would call you out on that and say that life experience isn't necessarily the same as being smart. So my tip is when the LSAT reading comprehension section has a question such as "the passage stated each of the following EXCEPT," then that means you have four paraphrases the LSAT considers kosher. Really look into these paraphrases and understand that these are other ways to say the same thing that was said in the passage, in proper LSAT language. This will help you understand the LSAT language and give you a huge boost in your overall score as well as your reading comprehension section.

TIP #170: FROM ROLF N., 179

My tip is about LSAT vocabulary. It's hard to develop vocabulary in a short period of time, so you will have to develop a different skill that is easier to learn. Of course, feel free to keep a list of words that give you a hard time because the LSAT often repeats words. The skill you need to develop is understanding the context. The way to do this is when you come across a word that you are unfamiliar with, don't look it up. Instead, do anything and everything you can to understand the word by looking at it in context. For example, if the LSAT says, 'This was a virtuous step towards democracy,' and you are not sure about the meaning of the word 'virtuous,' try to use the context. You probably know that democracy is a good thing, so 'virtuous' is probably a good thing when talking about taking a step in the direction of it. This skill will prove much more helpful than studying vocabulary. You can only learn a certain amount of words from now until the exam, but you can develop this skill that will help you with every word you are uncertain of.

TIP #171: FROM MINDY C., 175

I know by now that most of you will have heard about reading the *Economist* or the *Wall Street Journal* as a way of improving your reading comprehension. And while I agree, the tip I want to give you now is a bit more specific. There is one section in the *Wall Street Journal* and the *Economist* that will prove to be even more beneficial to your improvement and that is reading the letters to the author. These short nuggets of (usually) good writings are much more argumentative and require a bit more thought. So if you want to get a daily reading of outside materials, stick to the letters to the author.

TIP #172: FROM SARA O., 174

My tip will help those that are in need of reading faster because of the LSAT time constraints. While speed-reading is generally not recommended, reading faster than normal is. I found the best way to read faster without speed-reading is to read three words at a time. I also found that there is an amazing website that can help you with this. It is called 'Spreeder,' and it is basically an application that you can program to suit your needs. You program it to flash 3 words at a time, at 1000 per minute. Doing this about 10-15 minutes a day, for two weeks, helped me tremendously in speeding up my reading, and the best part was that I wasn't consciously doing so! I was simply reading faster by default. If you are a slow reader, you should definitely give this a shot!

TIP #173: FROM ELIJAH P., 175

One tip I want to share is something I learned about speed-reading. The technique is simple, so if you can practice it a bit, it will help you on those long reading comprehension passages. The idea is to start two or three words into the line and end two or three words before the end of the line. The words that you skipped, you glance at so quickly you don't spend almost any time on them. If you can practice this, it will speed up your reading by around 30%.

TIP #174: FROM CONNOR L., 175

My tip helped me improve my reading comprehension section by around 8 points! I really couldn't understand what I did wrong before, so I decided to break up the section into four bits, thereby doing one passage at a time. What was happening was that I was trying to save time by reading faster, and then I wouldn't have a good place to start when I got to the questions. I realized if I could dedicate the appropriate time to each passage, I would actually be able to read a bit slower, even reread the passage quickly, and answer all the questions, leaving question marks next to the ones I wasn't 100% sure about. That way, I could come back to them if I still had time left *on this specific passage*. The idea is to take each passage by itself and give it your all, instead of spreading the time among all the passages and not being able to come back to a passage without rereading the whole thing.

TIP #175: FROM ELLA T., 176

For me, the best way to approach reading comprehension passages was to simply make sure that I read the passage twice. I know many people will tell you this is a waste of time, but for me it worked. I would read the passage quickly the first time, and then read it very fast the second time around. This would give me the edge when it came to answering the questions. Also, because I was reading quite fast, I didn't have time to get caught up on being nervous or confused. Anything I didn't understand the first time, I was able to pick up on the second time.

Introduction to the
Test Day Tips

THIS NEXT SECTION IS ALL about how to handle test day and test day anxiety. I know that compared to your hours, weeks and months of studying, it might seem odd to devote a section in this book to just one day – but guess what? It's the only day that actually matters. You don't get points for studying; you get points for performance. Having a few techniques up your sleeve to enhance performance will prove to be really important.

Like the tips in the other sections, some of these will resonate with you more than others. You might find a handful you'll use, or maybe just one – but one that will make a huge difference.

Test day anxiety can be serious. Don't dismiss it until you've taken the LSAT and truly seen that it doesn't affect you. If you have seen the movie "Batman Begins" with Christian Bale, you'll recall the scene where the newly trained Bruce Wayne confronts his fear of bats. He doesn't deny it. He faces it. And that turns him into Batman.

I recommend a similar approach, although you won't need to train in the mountains with Master Ra's Al Ghul. If you're willing to admit you might get nervous during the LSAT, you can use the tips here to overcome, or at least minimize, your anxiety.

Good luck, and remember what Ducard told Bruce Wayne: "You must become more than just a man in the mind of your opponent."

Jacob

TIP #176: FROM CHARLOTTE H., 178

When you finish a section, even if you feel that it maybe didn't go exactly how you wanted it to go, forget about it! It's not the time to worry because now you need to focus on the next section and do your best. Besides, you might have done well in the section, sometimes you can actually do pretty good, even if you feel as though you haven't. So please don't waste your energy on worrying, instead, focus on the now.

TIP #177: FROM MAYA N., 176

This tip is about test day. I studied so much for the LSAT, I wanted to make sure everything was flawless on test day after putting in so much effort! I really wanted to find the perfect test site, a place where I could feel comfortable and be close enough so I wouldn't have to worry how to get there in the morning or where to find parking. I found a test site that was actually an hour from my house, but the test center was in a hotel, so I booked a room! I simply came the day before, relaxed, ate in their restaurant, swam in the pool and so on. I was able to totally relax and wake up much later in the morning than I would have needed to if I had to drive to the test site.

TIP #178: FROM PEYTON R., 177

So you've studied hard, taken time off work or school (or both) to study, and today is test day! My tip is about the morning of the test. I advise that you start going to sleep about an hour early every night, at least *three nights before!* So if you usually go to sleep at midnight, and the test is on Saturday, then go to sleep at 11pm on Wednesday, Thursday, and Friday night. The reason for this is it is hard to get a good night's sleep the night before the test, so get a few extra hours from the nights before, it will make it a lot easier.

TIP #179: FROM DOMINIC P., 175

On test day, I set up my watch and was excited to get started. I wasn't expecting any surprises. The clock hit 30 minutes, leaving 5 minutes to go. This is the time I leave for going back to some harder problems that I want to review, making sure that my answers are clearly written on the answer sheet, etc. I was waiting to hear the proctor yell out "5 minutes left," but instead, she called time and told us to close the books. I couldn't believe it! Luckily, there was one bold soul who raised his hand and politely said that he believed that there were still 5 minutes left. The proctor double-checked and apologized, leaving us with the final 5 minutes to finish. The lesson, is that if this does happen to you, while uncommon, don't be embarrassed to courteously raise your hand and tell them – it could very well save your test!

TIP #180: FROM MILES L., 180

You should also prepare well for the actual test setting. Wear comfortable clothes and shoes. I feel that you should be able, by this point, to do the test in your sleep, but there is no reason to add anything that might be uncomfortable to your day. I would also advise you to wear some sort of comfortable slippers, maybe something that you can take off under the table to relax a bit more. You know yourself better than anyone else does, you know what makes you relax, and you deserve it – you're taking the LSAT!

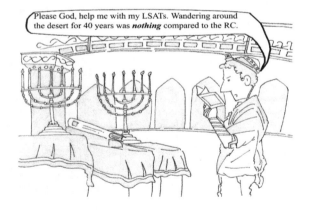

INTERVIEWS

WELCOME TO THE INTERVIEW SECTION of this book. From my survey with LSAT students from around the country, I collected the most important and pressing questions and handed them over to the nations' top LSAT instructors. They gave their awesome answers in the following outstanding interviews.

Interview with Nathan Fox

Jacob: We are extremely fortunate to have a very gifted and powerful LSAT instructor with us this morning. His name is Nathan Fox. Scoring 179 on his own LSAT, he attended UC Hastings in San Francisco. Today, Nathan teaches the LSAT full time in his own company, Fox Test Prep, also in San Francisco, and he loves his job. I personally have nicknamed him the LSAT Breaker, a term I borrowed from one of his amazing books *Breaking the LSAT,* which, by the way, is available on Amazon or on his website *foxtestprep. com*. With no further ado, welcome, Nathan.

Nathan: Hey, Jacob. Thanks for having me.

Jacob: It's great having you here. My first question for you this morning is: what would you say are the **underlying skills** that are needed to truly break the LSAT?

Nathan: Well, I think the LSAT is really testing two things, primarily. It's testing your reading ability and English language skills, and it's also testing how hard you can work. I can't help you much with the first part of that – a person's verbal skills take a long time to improve and, certainly just by studying the LSAT, you're going to get a little bit better at reading. That's the tough

107

part – sort of testing your natural ability to read – but the second thing is something that everybody can work on. You just have to put in the time and effort.

There are 69 practice tests available out there, and what I think they're doing is intentionally putting those practice tests out there to **reward people who are willing to actually sit there and do all of those practice tests.** So, probably, the most important thing that a student can do is realize that if they're taking the LSAT cold (without any preparation), they are probably doing the wrong thing because their competition is really working a lot harder. It's the kind of thing where people need to celebrate every one point increase and kind of grind it out. Some people are out there doing all 69 of those released practice tests. If you're not happy with your score, I would say, "Well, how many practice tests have you done?"

I think there's no substitute for hard work. Some people are going to be naturally better at the first part. You know, I was fortunate enough to be really strong in reading before I ever started the LSAT, and for the LSAT reading comprehension, I didn't have to do anything in order to score nearly 100%. I didn't need to prepare for the LSAT reading comprehension because I always already good at reading and comprehending, but for the logic games, for example, I had to do quite a bit of work to get better at them.

Then it was just a test of how good I am at forcing myself, every day, to sit there and do some practice. There's just no substitute for hard work.

Jacob: Right, that makes a lot of sense. Would you agree that it also depends on **which methods you use?**

Nathan: Of course. I mean, studying by yourself can be a waste of time. Again, it's better than nothing, but you can also burn up a lot of time by just kind of banging your head against the wall. So, certainly, I think that getting instruction from someone who you feel you can learn from is really, really helpful. There is also a lot of great books out there, as well as videos, DVDs, blogs and websites. There are a lot of places where you can get LSAT instruction.

I would recommend that students find a teacher who communicates with them in a way that they can understand, and, yeah, there isn't really one right methodology for the test. I think there's a lot of different ways of understanding it, but you can certainly benefit from working with an expert.

Jacob: What would you recommend for people who are just natural procrastinators?

Nathan: Well, I'm a natural procrastinator! I mean, hard work is not the thing that I'm best at. I think that as I've become older, **I've started to realize the value of doing a little bit every single day.** I think, sometimes, the thing that procrastinators tend to do is overestimate how long something is going to take or overestimate how painful something is going to be, and I've learned with myself, with exercise, for example, that I can just do some lightweight exercise every single day, like go for a walk. You know, I don't have to go into the gym for six hours on a Saturday if I just force myself to get outside and go for a little 30-45 minute walk every day.

I think studying for the LSAT works in exactly the same way. You know, I try to get my students to do maybe just one timed section every single day, and what I think students will do is they'll go, "Well, if I can't do a full test today, then it's not even worth my time." So they end up doing nothing instead of something. Does that make sense?

Jacob: Right. Yeah, I feel that procrastinators take the approach of – and I say this as a procrastinator myself – all or nothing. Like you said, if I can't do a full test and review every single question and get into depth with every single part, then I feel like there's no point in sitting down and studying at all.

Nathan: Yeah, and that's letting **the perfect be the enemy of the good**.

Jacob: Right.

Nathan: Instead of making some progress, you're just going to say, "Oh well, I can't do the perfect thing. So, I'll just not do anything at all."

Jacob: I know a lot of people that truly want to get into a good law school. There's so much information out there about admissions, and most of the admissions officers will tell you that it's really a numbers game. You know, the personal statement and letters of recommendation both come into play, but it only after you have the right numbers. So, ultimately, you really need a good LSAT score. Do you agree with that?

Nathan: Absolutely. Any law school admissions officer will tell you, "We look at every single component of every applicant's file." Maybe I'll take them for their word and believe that they will actually look at the personal statement of someone who applies with a really low LSAT score and a really low GPA, but I think there would have to be some shockingly good content in that personal statement to get them in.

This is a thought experiment that I like to drag my students through in my LSAT classes. Imagine you are in the admissions office of a school like UC Hastings, here in San Francisco. The year that I applied to Hastings, they had 6,000 applications for 400 spots in their class. Now, if you have 6,000 applications for 400 spots, aren't you going to make the first cut based on some numerical tool, for example, a spreadsheet with LSAT scores and GPA? I think you'd be stupid not to.

If you get 6,000 applications, you're going to have quite a few that have really good LSAT scores and GPA. So just to lighten your workload, why wouldn't you start from the top of that list?

So, bringing it back to the procrastination point, I see students spending way too much time on their personal statement. They're not yet where they want to be in their LSAT score, but they spend hours and hours agonizing about their personal statement and letters of recommendation, **instead of devoting that time to improving their LSAT score**. I really do believe that you need a sufficient LSAT score in order to get yourself in the game before they're even going to give your personal statement any serious consideration.

Jacob: Right. You can only apply to law school after you take the LSAT, and you only get your LSAT score at least three weeks after you take the test. So, even if you want to apply as soon as possible, you still have those three weeks, which is a nice amount of time to write one document.

Nathan: Yeah. I mean, it does take some students longer than three weeks to write their personal statement. What I tell people is, **if you have the energy for LSAT studying, you should probably be LSAT studying**. However, once in a while, you might need to take a little break from the LSAT books and do something to further your candidacy for law school. Well, that's a great time to do things like to write a really terrible first draft of your personal statement or send in the forms so that you can get your transcripts requested and sent to the LSAC.

I give my students a checklist of all these little things that they need to take care of. Taking care of those things is great. **Writing a terrible first draft as a personal statement is a necessary first step in order to write a good personal statement**, but yeah, I think you should put all that stuff after the LSAT because that's really the most important component.

Jacob: So, with that being said, students really understand that the LSAT is so important and yet will still procrastinate, and that is what my question was to begin with. We know it's important, and yet we still procrastinate, and that's an issue. So, I'm not sure – is there one answer for that or is it an individual thing?

Nathan: I really love the idea of just doing a little something every single day. I think habits are really important. **I think you need to make LSAT studying a daily habit,** just like exercise, flossing your teeth, or anything else that you need to take care of on a given day. I think LSAT studying needs to rise to that level of, 'I'm committed to doing this', so that it becomes part of your daily routine.

I think it might be painful at first, but if your goal is only to do half an hour or one 35-minute section, maybe that's not so daunting as to keep you from actually doing it. You know, it's like, "Hey, in 35 minutes, I'm going to be done with this and then I can go back to watching whatever crappy TV show I was going to watch." That's fine. You've just got to take care of that little 35-minute burst first.

So, I think having a daily routine is the most important part.

Jacob: Okay, that's great. That's a really great tip. So, that leads to my second question. You mentioned the fact that there are a lot of printed LSATs out there, and we talked about the procrastination aspect – that people actually need to sit down and study. When they in fact do sit down to study, what is the difficulty? Why is it so hard for people, even if they study, to get the score they want or even to improve at all?

Nathan: I think it's different for everybody. I have several different answers for that question. The first reason, and I hate to dash people's dreams, but it's really hard for people who don't have strong English skills. I think it's always going to be hard if you don't have strong English skills. **The truth about law is that lawyers are**

equivalent to gladiators, and the weapon they use to do battle with is the English language.

So if you're somebody who finds that when you're doing an LSAT practice test, that you're running into many words that you don't understand, I think you have an uphill battle with this test. I'm not saying you can't do it. I'm just saying it's probably going to be harder for you than it is for other people. There are some people who sit down and they know every single word on the test. These people already have an enormous advantage over you.

Beyond that, I think another reason why it's so tough for people is maybe because they don't recognize how much work there is to be done. Again, there are 69 released practice tests, and if you just strove to get one more question right on every single test you took, and if you did enough tests, you would definitely reach your goal. I'll see a student and they'll tell me they haven't improved, and I'll say, "Well, your first score was 142 and you got 146 in the latest test you did. So, going from 142 to 146 is a nice improvement."

The scale only goes from 120 to 180. There's only a 60 point scale. So, if you move up four points, you've moved up a significant chunk of that scale. However, students still get discouraged. They feel like they want it all right now, and I think that's a pretty big barrier. One reason why people get disappointed is because they don't recognize when they are actually making progress.

You know, it's a good experiment. If the test went from 1200 to 1800, instead of going from 120 to 180, then people might have improved 40 points instead of improving 4 points, and it sounds like a lot more. So, I do think there's a sort of psychological block, there, for a lot of people.

Jacob: That would be interesting. Yeah, I don't know if the LSAC really cares about people's psychological health. I've heard from

Noah Teitelbaum that if you take one practice test and score 150 and then you take another test and score 150 again, while you maybe didn't improve, you at least locked in that score, so to speak. You know you can get at least 150, and now you can strive to get higher.

Nathan: Right. And the other thing is that people don't normally go down. So, if I see a student go from 140 to 141, I'm happy because it usually means that they have learned something. I don't usually see students take any steps backwards. Now, there's all that noise in the data that anyone's test can be plus or minus five points, but if you do go up a little bit, then you get that same score again and that same score again – that indicates that you have achieved a new level of scoring. That's something people should take as a positive and they should try to get excited about that, instead of feeling discouraged. Instead, they want more in every single test and that's just not realistic.

Jacob: Would you agree that there comes a point where, especially with the logic games, **where it kind of all kicks in**? When I was a kid, there was that famous Winnie the Pooh movie where Winnie the Pooh gets stuck in the rabbit hole. For days, they're trying to pull him out, but he ate so much honey and gained weight that he can't get out of the hole. Then, one day, rabbit leans on him, and Winnie the Pooh budges. Then they were able to pull him out. I think that something similar happens with the logic games, or even with the logical reasoning too.

Nathan: More so for logic games than for logical reasoning, I think. On logical reasoning, the games tend to be incremental, like one more question per week. You know, that should be your goal for logical reasoning. **Understand a little bit more every day**.

On the logic games, it is like the metaphor you used. It makes sense. You might not improve within a week, or two or three, but then, all of a sudden, I'll see students jump by six questions on the logic games. Just like, boom, they get one more whole game correct!

So, on the games, for sure, your gains will happen in leaps and bounds all at once. It's like riding a bike, too. When you first try to ride a bike, you just crash and crash and you can't feel it. You're like, "This is impossible!" But then one day, all of a sudden, you just ride down the street, and you go, "Wow! That was not at all difficult, really."

That's exactly what I see with pretty much every student and logic games. It takes everybody a different amount of time, but I pretty much have every student practicing them at one point and making big leaps in logic games.

Jacob: Okay. That's good to know because, like you said, a lot of people get discouraged from doing a few games and not seeing a huge improvement right away. So, they need to know that it takes time. Hopefully, they can wait for that surge in their score and work towards that goal. In other words, **don't work towards getting a perfect score the first time, but understand that it comes in increments.**

Nathan: Yeah, absolutely.

Jacob: Okay. So, that being said, when it comes to logical reasoning, I've heard from a lot of people that they seem to hit a barrier once they get to the 20-21 mark. In other words, they get 20 or 21 correct out of the last section, which is 25 or 26 usually, and they just can't seem to get past that point. What would your advice for those kinds of students be?

Nathan: Yeah, that's pretty strong. Missing 4 out of 25? That's pretty good, and I've worked with quite a few of those high-scoring students. **The key is, of course, to review your misses. You should also be reviewing your guesses too.** I think that's one thing that students don't quite get: the reviewing. Sometimes they narrow it down to two answers and pick B instead of D, and the answer actually turns out to be B. So the answer they gave did actually turn out to be right, so they don't bother reviewing it, but they still don't really understand why B was better than D. They kind of just got lucky. If you continue to do that, then you're going to continue to get those kinds of 50/50 questions. Sometimes, you'll get them right. Sometimes, you'll get them wrong. So, you should review the ones you missed, and you should review the ones where you guessed or semi-guessed.

Obviously, try to recognize what types of questions you're missing most often because you will probably need someone to explain that to you. That can be a study partner or a professional, but you need someone to tell you exactly why the right answer is right and the wrong answers are wrong. If it makes sense when someone explains it to you, and when I say make sense, **it makes sense enough that you could explain it to someone else**, that's when the light bulb is really on. If that happens, then you've learned, and maybe you're going to make that same mistake a few times, but you shouldn't make it 10 more times.

So, I think that's really the process. It's the same process I would recommend for low scorers and high scorers. It's just to achieve the understanding of one more question, one more question, and then that'll move you forwards.

Jacob: Nathan, would you recommend making a list of questions that you got wrong? Let's say all the questions that you got wrong in the 20s and 30s, and then reviewing all those questions?

Nathan: No, I don't think I would do that. My personal style is that when I'm done with a test, I'm pretty much done with the test. There are so many tests out there, that's what I would do (and this is how I work with my private tutoring students and the students in my classes) is just doing the test, then talk about the ones we don't quite understand, and we turn on as many light bulbs as we possibly can. Then we move on.

There's 71 tests. So, I'd rather apply what we've learned to a new test rather than rehash old tests. The other thing is that some questions are just not that well written. They're not all perfect; this is not very scientific. So, I think you just do the questions and learn what you can from them. Sometimes you're going to go, "Oh geez, I can't believe I did that. Okay, I'll never do that again!"

Some questions you may not be able to get total clarity on why the right answer is right and why the wrong answers are wrong, and that's fine, too. You gave it a shot. You didn't get it fully? That's fine. Move on. You'll get the next one.

Jacob: What do you have to tell us about questions that were removed from the LSAT?

Nathan: When you look at the old tests, they sometimes remove an item from scoring. This will actually change people's scores. It's pretty rare that they do that, though.

Jacob: Yeah, there have been seven questions (to date) that the LSAT has removed and, like you said, it's mostly in the old ones.

Nathan: It does seem like they have improved at writing the questions. When you read the really old tests, there are more questions that I kind of disagree with. On the newer tests, for example: June 2013, I thought every question on the test was perfectly fair.

Jacob: Okay, that's good to know. Hopefully, that'll give some encouragement to the people still to take their test. So, I wanted to ask you another question. You wrote, on your blog, your list of the 10 LSAT commandments, which I think is something that everybody should post on their wall in front of their study desks at home! One of them is "Thou shalt point a gun to thine own head," and I feel that this is a great part of your philosophy when it comes to studying. So, if you could, please elaborate on that a little bit?

Nathan: Sure, Jacob. So this tip applies to logic games. On logic games, you need to realize that **there is a single objectively correct answer to every single question**. The right answer is objectively right, and the wrong answers are objectively wrong. A computer could solve the logic games with 100% accuracy.

There's no guessing. No semi-guessing, no figuring out which answer is the best of the five answers, no 'best' answer. There is only one correct answer and four incorrect answers. So, when I say to put a gun to your own head, I want students to answer logic game questions with 100% certainty, and if I can just get them to do that, **if I can just get them to slow down** and answer the questions with certainty, **then they start to realize that the test is actually quite easy.**

You will never get better at the games if you don't learn to answer the questions with 100% certainty. Students panic at the time and they felt like, "Well, I have to hurry because if I don't hurry, then I'm not going to finish." Well, the truth is, and this is a paradox of the LSAT, **you need to actually slow down to see how the test is easy to eventually go faster.**

Jacob: That's a paradox, right? You need to slow down to speed up.

Nathan: It's a paradox, but I think it's absolutely true. If you go fast, you make silly mistakes. You misunderstand things. You don't make the connections between the rules. So it's not surprising that the questions look really hard. You end up taking forever on each question; you try to go fast, but you just crash.

If you take it the other way, you slow down. You calm down. You may read the rules a couple more times to make sure you really get them. You notice that there's a connection between a couple of the rules and every time you make one of those connections, you've learned something new about the way the game works. Then, when you finally get to the questions, the questions look easy to you. You breeze through the questions and, before you know it, you're on to the next game. That only happens if you slow down and go for accuracy first. **Accuracy leads to speed, not the other way around.**

Jacob: I saw a few of the logic games that you've explained in the free videos that you have on your website, and it sounds like exactly what you've said here. It's very clear. I've heard that idea that you need to slow down in order to speed up, but the way that you do it yourself shows how true it is.

Nathan: Thank you, Jacob. I love what I do. I've been doing this for years now, and it's a weird little niche. I never thought that I would spend my life teaching the LSAT. So, sure, I'm just trying to tell it like it is. I think students overcomplicate it and, frankly, a lot of the people out there selling LSAT classes and books also overcomplicate it. These people pump themselves up by trying to make it look hard. I just don't think that's a very good way to teach. I think there's a better way to just show students how easy it actually is. So, on the first night of my classes, I'm at the board and I'm doing logic games. It looks so easy and by the end of class they've all realized, "Oh, it actually is easy."

That's what I'm going for. I love teaching – it's fun to see people's eyes light up and go, "Oh, man. I can't believe that's all there was to it. It's just not that big of a deal!"

Jacob: Right, right. So, going back to the former question that I asked, and why the LSAT is so challenging to so many people. Maybe that would also be a good answer – because people overcomplicate it.

Nathan: I think so, definitely. That's just a great example of where I think I can help students sometimes, by just getting them to strip away all of the crappy techniques and strategies that they are applying because all of that stuff is actually *preventing* them from understanding.

Jacob: You know, when people read a magazine, even if it's the Economist, where the English is a little bit more complicated than People Magazine – nobody's underlining things. Nobody's taking notes.

Nathan: When you get done reading that article in the Economist, you are able to close the magazine and turn to a friend and say, "Yeah, this article is generally about XYZ." If you can do that, if you can tell a friend what an article is generally about, then you've done all you need to do because most of the questions on the reading comprehension are really related to the bigger picture. Did you comprehend the bigger picture or not?

Now, of course, there's going to be some detailed questions that are going to require you to look back at the passage again, but that's fine. You weren't supposed to memorize the passage. It's not called reading memorization. It's called reading comprehension. Did you get the bigger picture? Do you kind of know what's there? If you did, then you can usually manage the questions pretty easily.

Law school is intensely related to verbal abilities and reading abilities. That's a really cool parenting thing. I tell students to read whatever they want to read. **To read anything that keeps you reading is the best thing that you could be reading.** So, if you want to read about sports – fantastic! If you want to read about arts, dance, music, whatever it is that you're into, read that.

When I was in high school, I read every book that Stephen King ever wrote. People are probably going to say, "Stephen King is a trash novelist." Whatever. I was into it. It was fun and I kept turning the pages, and it's those pages that I turned 20 years ago that made me the reader that I am now.

Jacob: Right. It's all English after all. I actually have a friend who just graduated from Columbia. He scored around the high 170s, I think 178, and I also asked him about the reading comprehension. He had the same answer. He said, "In high school, I was always reading: just novels, science fiction and stuff like that. If you can read science-fiction novels, any novels, you'll be fine with the LSAT."

So, as I've said before, I'm very impressed with your teaching methods and abilities. So, students can go to your website at foxtestprep.com and see some of your free videos. Is that correct?

Nathan: Yeah, they can see the first 15 hours of my online class. It's a 55 hour class in total that covers 20 full-length LSAT tests, but I made the first 15 hours of it free, the idea being that I wanted people to go and try out the class, not just for sale purposes. I wanted them to actually be able to learn from those first 15 hours and hopefully share it with their friends. So, the first 15 hours are freely available. I think it covers four or five full LSAT tests. That would be plenty to decide if you like my style or not, and then, if you want to go with the full class after that, I'd love to have you do that as well.

Jacob: So, one thing I noticed, besides your teaching style, is that there are live videos – you're taking videos out of real classes that you taught. I obviously advocate your method of showing a live class, but what was your motivation behind that? Because I'm sure it is hard to produce, having to fix the lights right and everything. It's probably a lot easier to make a video with just the audio. So, what was your motivation for doing it that way?

Nathan: Yeah, I just thought it would be fun! My primary goal as an LSAT teacher is to keep people awake. I don't know how students do it! They come to class after a long day of work, a long day of school, or a long day of work *and* school, and then they show up at 6 o'clock on Tuesdays and Thursdays for full four-hour LSAT classes. I don't think I would be able to get through it myself.

So, I feel like my job is to keep it lively, sprinkle in a few swear words here and there to try to keep people paying attention. If I can get a couple of laughs, that's great. So, I wanted my online class to embody that exact same experience, and the only way I could think of doing that was just to actually record one of my real classes. So when you look at my online class, it's just as if you're sitting in the back row of one of those real LSAT classes.

Jacob: Well, you can either keep it lively or give them a Starbucks gift card...

Nathan: I don't think coffee's that powerful! I think the LSAT can defeat any level of caffeine! The wrong LSAT instructor, I'm sure, reading to you out of a book... you can have a triple shot of whatever and it's probably not going to get the job done.

Jacob: Nathan, like you said in the beginning of our conversation, people should, and they do, put a lot of emphasis and a lot of weight on the LSAT and their LSAT score. After that, they can get into a good law school and find a great job, etc.

So you would think that in itself would keep people up, but it seems to be the case that the LSAT can get so boring, especially the technicalities of it, like assumptions, formal logic etc. When you look at that, you're not thinking about your future law career. So like you said, you need to find a way to stay awake.

I have one more question, and this might be the most important part. You've been teaching the LSAT for a number of years now. You, yourself, scored a 99th percentile score. So, as far as LSAT prep goes, **if you have one tip for everybody, for our listeners and our readers, what would that one tip be?**

Nathan: Jacob, I mentioned this one before, but what I think is really important is to **do a little bit every day**. Beyond that, I think my other number one tip would be **just don't do it alone**. I think that a lot of students don't have the resources for a class or private tutors. That's fine, but there's nothing stopping you from getting a study partner.

When I studied, I actually worked with a study partner, not a professional. I had some books, I had some good printed materials, but it made my prep much more tolerable when I had a friend who was also studying for the test. All we did was meet once a week and have coffee. We would do a test, and we would meet for coffee and discuss that test. If I didn't understand something, she would explain it to me. If she didn't understand something, I would explain it to her, and that was perfectly effective for studying.

Now, sure, working with a professional would have been more efficient.

Jacob: Maybe one point more efficiently.[4]

Nathan: Yeah. I mean, it would have been better, but it wouldn't have been drastically better. It was really nice because it kept me doing my stuff. I had to do my homework. I had to show up at the café, get a cup of coffee, sit down, and talk about the test.

Jacob: It sounds like an accountability partner in a way.

Nathan: And the accountability was great. As far as learning-wise, she happened to be someone who was scoring at a far lower level than I was, and I think a lot of people would say, "Well, I'm not going to study with somebody who's not up to my standards." In fact, when you get to law school, you'll see people who have study groups where you're not invited to be in the study group if you didn't score above 165 on the LSAT. All eyes on the LSAT score!

Jacob: Oh, really?

Nathan: Yup, it's ridiculous like that. I mean, that's obviously not

---

4 Nathan scored a 179. JE

the study group that you even want to be in, right? If they admitted you, you would not want to be in that silly group! Anyway, I studied with a girl who was scoring 30 points lower than I was. I think a lot of people would be like, "That's a waste of my time. I'm not going to do that," but I learned so much by explaining stuff to her.

For example, there might have been a question that I got right, and in explaining to her how and why I got it right, I learned much better than I knew it to begin with. So, a study partner, I think, is highly valuable.

If you can pay for a tutor or if you can pay for a class, that's fantastic. But even if you have a tutor or a class, I think you should also get yourself a study partner.

Jacob: Right. I was just going to say that because it seems like there are advantages to having a study partner that you might not get with a tutor. Even if they're at the same score as you, even if you're just explaining something to them and they already know what you're talking about, I think that would be beneficial as well. That would be more helpful. So, it seems like there's a lot of benefits to having a study partner.

Nathan: Somebody at a higher level is going to teach you stuff you didn't know. Somebody at a lower level, however, will help you to solidify your understanding by explaining to them the things that you do know. You're going to watch them make mistakes, and you're going to go, "I'm going to make sure not to make that mistake." So, yeah, I think it's really valuable.

Jacob: Right, and that makes sense that that's your number-one tip because it really encompasses everything. In other words, no matter what methods you use, no matter what material you have, no matter how long you have studied, having a study partner makes sure that you stick to it, and I think that's a really great tip. Thank you for that.

So yeah, I think that concludes our conversation for today. I want to thank you, Nathan, for joining us. I'm sure that a lot of students are going to derive **a lot of valuable information** from our conversation, and I also urge students who are listening or reading this to stop reading or listening to this and go over to **foxtestprep. com**! Watch the free videos, read the blog. There's also a lot of free information on the blog there, so that you can get a taste of the philosophy behind the course. Then, sign up for the course!

Nathan, I've reviewed a lot of these different websites, and I really feel that you're one of the top five, not ranking them one to five, but I just have a top five in my head. I think you are, for sure, up there in the top five, so thank you again for joining us.

Nathan: Thank you, Jacob. Yeah, it was a lot of fun.

Jacob: Thank you Nathan.

Nathan: Take care, thanks.

INTERVIEW WITH MARY ADKINS

Jacob: Mary Adkins is a Yale law school graduate, an incredible LSAT tutor and above all an awesome person. We are super lucky to get her on this interview today to answer students' questions. Hello, Mary!

Mary: Hi, Jacob!

Jacob: How are you this morning?

Mary: I'm doing great. How are you?

Jacob: I'm great. Thank you so much for joining us. I'm sure that our listeners and readers will benefit a lot from this interview. After all, you are a **top** LSAT tutor. So, my first question for you, Mary, is how do you motivate your students to study for the LSAT?

Mary: Usually, *I scream at them...* Just kidding, I don't scream! That's a good question. I find it really beneficial to explain, at the beginning of my work with someone, that the LSAT is a really teachable test, and that's something that I really like about it, by the way. It's something I like about the test in itself, and it is one of the things I really like about teaching it.

126

It's an aptitude test, in the sense that it's evaluating one's ability to think and read and write logically, but those are skills that can be learned. And that's an exciting thing for someone teaching the test, and I think for people learning the test too, especially when they start off not scoring close to where they want to score. I've seen students' scores go up 10-15 points pretty regularly because of the nature of the test.

In terms of motivating them, I find this to be an encouraging conversation to have, but in my experience, students are pretty motivated themselves. I find my role to be focused on other areas than on providing motivation. I mean, the LSAT is given so much weight by law schools that, for the most part, students come in wanting to do really well and eager to do the work to get them scoring what they want to score.

Jacob: Like you said, law school itself is a big motivator. What would you tell a student who says, "I have the homework you gave me, I know what to do, but I just start to procrastinate."

Mary: You know, I think I've had that situation so rarely! However, when it does come up, I think I just take a tough love approach, like, "You're going to have to sit down and do it. Let's figure out how this is going to happen." So, it's really a practical kind of approach like, "Let's do what we need to do. Let's make a schedule. Let's figure out where you're going to go." I mean, if the problem is it's loud at home, then let's try to find another location. Let's look at library hours. Let's do something so that we have a concrete plan and, generally, I find that people, more or less, can stick to that if they're really motivated. If they're not really motivated, I'm not sure if any conversation with me is going to change that, you know?

Jacob: I've heard of students who wanted to become more motivated, so they would go and visit law schools. They would go and visit a law school, especially a law school that has nice scenery, you know, maybe a fancy library, just to see something that will get them motivated and force them to realize, "If I want to get here, I'm going to have to study.

Mary: Right. I mean, that sounds like a good idea just to get them excited about it. I remember a friend I had in college. She was taking the LSAT while we were in college, and she was studying for it. I had never looked at an LSAT before, but I remember she would go over to Duke, the law school, to study in the law school library, and now I wonder if it was the same kind of thing, like getting herself excited about it.

Jacob: I hear about students who think that they have such a unique story to tell in their personal statement, so they believe that the personal statement will mitigate any low LSAT score or any low GPA, and it seems like, from what I hear, it's just not the case. It can help once in a while, but it's not something to count on. Would you agree?

Mary: Yeah, for sure. I mean, there's very little you can do to compensate for a low LSAT score. It's just got so much weight on it. As a threshold matter, I mean, of course the application, as a whole, matters in many circumstances, but if you have an LSAT below the threshold at which a particular school is really willing to consider you as a viable candidate, then your personal statement may still be incredible, but the odds of it pulling the weight for the whole application are small.

Jacob: Okay, so I guess we're motivated now! My next question for you, Mary, is **what should one's goals be when studying for the LSAT?**

Mary: I think a misconception that people often have is that they can improve their LSAT score by learning tricks, and the reason I think that's so dangerous is it's only going to get you so far. I mean, there are certain patterns to the test and we can teach those patterns. People can learn what to look for and how to spot an extreme term and a wrong answer choice, **but unless you really understand the underlying skills that the test is designed to evaluate, your score isn't going to be in the top percentile.**

So, I'd say the goal should not be learning tricks, but learning what the test is designed to test: your ability to think logically. The goal should be to come up to that threshold and become a more logical, attuned, precise thinker. That's the best thing you can do to be better at the LSAT, but the beauty of this is that it's not just going to make you better at the LSAT – **it's going to make you a better logical thinker overall, which will make you a better student and a better lawyer.**

Jacob: Right. That's what I always say, people need to realize that studying for the LSAT will help them, not just on the exam, but in life generally. In other words, it's not just a short-term goal. It's really a long term one. We were talking before about motivation. The fact that it's long term, in itself, can be a big motivator. We know that there are pre-law courses out there, but someone could just study for the LSAT to improve their reading and logic, you know?

Mary: Yeah. I'd say that your goal should be to become a more logical thinker, a more attuned thinker, and a precise thinker.

Jacob: Yeah. I would recommend people print that out and put it in front of their desks. I know that when you have a goal and you actually achieve it, there's an immense sense of accomplishment and a huge boost to your self-esteem. It's a lot better to achieve a goal in that way than just to achieve it without having planned it before.

So, if your goal is to become a more logical thinker, it'll show in your LSAT score, will it not?

Mary: I believe it would. I was just going to say, as a tutor and teacher, of course I'm very excited when my students reach their goal scores or when my students see a lot of improvement, but one of my most rewarding moments, as a teacher, was when one of my students, at the end of the course, told me that he felt smarter having taken it. That's exactly what we're going for. **It's like an overall improvement in thinking ability**. One way that's manifested is in the LSAT, but it's not exclusive to the LSAT.

Jacob: That sounds accurate. There's the famous Wall Street Journal article[5] that talks about research that shows that studying for the LSAT does actually improve your intelligence. It was a three month-based research, and that proves your point because studying for the LSAT makes you smarter. If you couldn't get smarter from studying, how could your scores go up?

Mary: Right.

Jacob: So, that all ties in nicely. And, again, becoming a more logical thinker, like you said, will help you in law school. That way, I think, is a really good way to put it because that way students can see that it's not just about taking the LSAT and finishing it – taking the LSAT really is a form of preparation for law school.

Mary: Yeah, exactly. **It's going to make them better law students.** I'm with you. I can see that as being a great motivation. This is not only going to help you get into law school. This is going to help you once you're there, and this is going to help you think more logically for the rest of your life.

Jacob: So, if that's the case, you'll see advice on different websites about studying for the LSAT and one of the tips you will always see is **not to cram for the LSAT**. You know, you can't study three weeks before the test and expect to get anywhere. You really have

5 Aug 28, 2012

to take your time, and, you know, if it's a matter of becoming a more logical thinker, then nobody's getting smarter in two or three weeks. Even with intensive study, you're not going to change your brain chemistry in three weeks. It will take at least a few months to change your thought patterns.

Mary: Exactly. I mean, I think there are people who are able to do that though – I know some of them. I went to law school with most of them, but the people who are able to study, to begin and finish studying for the LSAT in two to three weeks, are the people who already have the full groundwork in their brains. It's already laid. The neurological pathways are already there. They are already logical thinkers in the way the test demands.

So what they're really doing is learning the content. They're accumulating knowledge like, "What am I going to see on the test? Let me prepare for it in that way," but they're not actually changing the way they think.

Jacob: Right, right. So, that being said, **how long would you recommend studying for, as far as being able to change your thinking?**

Mary: It's so specific to the person, so it's really hard to say, to be honest. I think several months, at least. To be safe, you should give yourself several months. I wanted to bring this up at some point, actually, because my colleague, Matt Sherman, has a brilliant response to the idea that you can peak too soon when it comes to the LSAT – he thinks it's a myth.

There is no peaking too soon: **you only get better at the LSAT the longer you study it**. You don't get worse. So, starting as far in advance as possible, in that view, would be beneficial. I mean, life's realities make that impossible for most of us. We're not going to study the LSAT for years, but if we did, we would be better at it when we finally took it. So, several months is kind of the general answer that I would give to that question, but even students starting to study two or three months in advance find that they're really under a lot of pressure. They're trying to do too much in a really short amount of time.

So, even 3-4 months in advance is still putting a lot of pressure on yourself, particularly if you have other obligations, like work or school, **but I find students tend to find six months in advance much more manageable**. Again, six months is not always long enough for them to see as much improvement as they want. So, that's when it really becomes person-specific. Some students will have to postpone because they can tell that they're not quite ready.

Jacob: So, your general advice is to give it time, not rush it, because it's really a matter of changing your whole thought process and not just learning tricks. So, again, it's different for every person, but the student should know how long it takes them and how much time they'll have to devote to it... those kind of factors.

So, we're talking about how the LSAT really can increase intelligence and how that is another motivator, I would say, because who doesn't want to be smarter? If that's the case, would it counter the argument I hear all the time that the LSAT is simply not fair? There are questions that are so abstract – some claim that "the LSAT is not fair, and that's why I can't do it." How would you argue with that?

Mary: I would say that the LSAT is about as fair as tests get. A mantra we repeat throughout the curriculum at Manhattan LSAT is to be literal. **Think literal**. Say it literal, and when you have a test for which that's a suitable mantra, it's a sign that it's a pretty fair test. So, to generalize here, it's not a test asking you to read between the lines or bring in outside knowledge based on life experience, when all of our life experiences vary. It's asking you things like

"Which of the following does the passage state or not state?" It's something that's literally there or literally not.

So, really, it's quite a fair test. I guess one could argue that it's not fair in the sense that it does demand an ability to think in a certain way – to infer logically and to deduct logically – but it doesn't purport to be anything else. I mean, that's what the test is, and that's its strength, in my view.

Jacob: Right, and that's what you need to get into law school anyway. So, if that's not fair, then what's going to happen in law school, right?

Mary: Exactly.

Jacob: Right. I know this might be a whole other conversation, but I've seen a reading comprehension passage in one of the 20s. It talks about people who are afraid of the side effects of medication, but they're not afraid of much bigger hazards. The idea was that people are afraid of small things when they should be afraid of the bigger things. Then, the question asked you to make an analogy of what the passage was talking about, and the correct answer was an analogy of a person that dodges in and out of traffic. In other words, they're not careful of real dangers, but they're really afraid of getting hit by a meteor. So, I thought there was some outside knowledge there that you needed to use because you needed to know that getting hit by a meteorite is very uncommon.

So, would that be an example of kind of bending the rules as far as bringing outside knowledge in?

Mary: I think that's actually a **good illustration of the level of outside knowledge that the LSAT does ask of you,** but I think it's also a good illustration of how the reading comprehension part of the test can be taught. What we teach is that students should work from wrong to right to eliminate wrong answer choices, as opposed to searching the answer choices for the correct one first, the reason being that in a question like that, it's an analogy. An analogy is not a scientific sort of entity, right? It's literal. It's going to have factors that are similar to the situation that you've been given and factors that are dissimilar because it's not identical.

What you're looking for is the best analogy. So, one way of doing that is to eliminate the ones that are more dissimilar than the remaining ones, and on reading comprehension, that is the most reliable process. But I do see how that question demands outside knowledge. You have to know that the chances of getting hit by meteors are pretty small, and the chances of getting into a car accident are pretty high. Even if you didn't know that, if the other four answer choices had some reason why they're clearly more off base than that last one, which you're unsure about, then it's still possible to get it right.

Jacob: Awesome, yeah. I've had that question for a while. It just came back to me when you brought up the idea of not bringing in outside knowledge. I'm happy we got to that because that's an important philosophy that you're teaching at Manhattan LSAT, of going from wrong to right.

So, my next question for you, Mary, is **what is the number one mistake students make when studying for the LSAT?**

Mary: I would say that believing that quantity equals quality. Often, people think that by doing more questions, they will just inherently improve, but it's like with anything else: practice doesn't make perfect; *'perfect practice makes perfect'* as Vince Lombardi said. So, to teach yourself to do well on the LSAT, you need to teach yourself to do one question well. What does that mean?

It means taking the question apart, dissecting not only the problem and the correct answer, but the wrong ones too, looking for patterns and question types, being attuned to your own thinking process and being aware of what is aiding you or holding you back. I categorize all of these tasks as *quality*. They take more time. They take more attention. They're more difficult, to be honest, than just pulling out the next test and flying through it, but it's worth it.

Jacob: One student I know went through all the LSATs twice and scored 174. That might sound like good advice, but the thing is there are so many variables. I don't know where he was scoring initially. He might have started at 170, and going through the LSATs, he gained 4 more points. So, you never know. But I'm going to take your professional advice over that and conclude that going over the questions themselves doesn't have as much impact as studying the skills. Is that more or less what you said?

Mary: Yeah, and in that example with that student, I'm not saying that quantity cannot be immensely beneficial. I mean, the more you do the better, by all means, but what I'm saying is that it shouldn't be substituted for quality. So, sufficient review time has to be factored into the overall amount of time that you dedicate to LSAT study.

Jacob: Right. So, that's awesome. I know I only asked you for the number-one mistake, but what would you say is the number two, the second most common mistake that students make? Obviously, I'm asking these questions so that people can avoid these mistakes.

Mary: Right. I would say the second mistake students make is that they **aren't very strict on timing their own practice**, and they think that whatever they score when they're giving themselves three or four extra minutes here and there is an accurate reflection of the score they will get when they go in. It's very common and I understand the compulsion to do that. You think, "Oh, I'm almost done with this game. I'm going to give myself a few more minutes."

You know, in some cases, it's good to do that. Give yourself a few more minutes, finish the game. Learn how to do the game, but don't think that what you scored on that logic game section is what you are "scoring" on logic games. You know what I mean?

Jacob: So, in other words, you're saying that the timing is not something that's separate from the logic, reading or the setups of games. It's an essential part of it. In other words, a logic game is a logic game when you're timing it. Otherwise, it's just a game.

Mary: Exactly. And I throw that out there, too, because it's sad to see someone disappointed because they expected to do much better than they ended up doing because they were essentially giving themselves untimed conditions when they were practicing. Then they go in and do it under timed conditions, and it's a rude awakening.

Jacob: Those are two really good tips. Speaking of going from wrong to right, I think that's exactly what we were just doing by looking at the mistakes students make, in order not to make them. Going from the wrong way, in that sense: the wrong way to study, to the right way to study.

Awesome, this is really great material, Mary. I really appreciate this. Everybody reading and listening to this is going to have a wakeup call from these two tips.

Mary: I hope so!

Jacob: So, my next question is: how do you respond when someone tells you that they are simply not a good test taker? In fact, do you mind if I give my own answer, first?

Mary: Sure.

Jacob: Some people say, "I understand the logic. I can do the games and I can read – I'm just not a good test taker!" And then they go on: "I don't need to study. I shouldn't study because, anyway,

I'm not a good test taker. So, what's the point?" So, my answer, and tell me if you agree, is what I told someone recently, actually not about the LSAT. He was talking about the GMAT, to go to business school. He told me that he is simply not a good test taker. I told him, "Look, if they gave you a test of the names and birthdays of your siblings, and the names and occupations of your parents, and where you went to elementary, high school, college and your current job, your boss's name, etc., you would answer those questions with 100% accuracy, and you would not say 'I'm not a good test taker', right?"

The reason for that is because you know the information *so well* that it doesn't matter if it's a computerized test, a written test, if it's under time or if the guy next to you has fallen asleep and is snoring. When you know that information so well, that excuse all of a sudden disappears into thin air.

That's my answer, but what's your take on that concept?

Mary: Well, I really like that answer, and I think I would add a layer to it and say that the reason you would be so good at that test is not just that you know the answers to all those questions, but also because **you know that you know** the answers to all those questions. So, you go in with the confidence that you have no problem giving the birthday of your sister because you know that it's November 7th, or whenever.

Even if you went into the test knowing the answers to the questions, if you weren't sure that you knew them, you could still be a "bad test taker" because acute anxiety just gets in the way of performing optimally. So, I have had to deal with this in a couple of ways because of my students before.

I explain to people that it's a teachable test and that they can improve, which is true. I think as they see themselves improving and see themselves actually learning the underlying skills, their confidence goes up, and confidence going up goes a long way to starting to believe that you can take the test and do well in it.

I also try to teach how to reduce anxiety levels, so they can learn the ways they might try to reduce stress outside of just an LSAT prep test or course book. So, exercise, yoga or meditation is good. These are some tried and tested ways that people deal with anxiety, and these are things that I like to recommend to my students.

Jacob: That's good advice. That kind of brings us right into my next question, and I'm actually looking at the blog on Manhattan LSAT, at an article you wrote titled "Achievement on the LSAT as State of Mind." You explain over there how the state of mind and your confidence can help LSAT performance. So, could you say a little bit about that and explain why it's so important?

Mary: Basically, what I was writing about there, it's along very similar lines to what I just said. It's kind of a power positive thinking point. You feel around you all the time, especially if you look for it, that people who believe in themselves do well and people who don't, don't. I don't mean to over simplify here. The LSAT fits right into this pattern, along with other challenges. It's kind of like, remember a few years ago, the book *The Secret* came out? There was a craze. Oprah talked about it. It's the idea of the law of attraction. It's going to be very difficult to do extremely well on the LSAT unless you're capable of believing that you can do extremely well on the LSAT.

It's going to be hard to sit there and be calm for four hours unless you really believe that you can sit there and be calm for four hours. In other words, **if you view yourself as a terrible test taker, the chance that you're not going to be a good test taker are much higher than they would be if you really became convinced that you're capable of doing well on the test**.

Jacob: And if you read some autobiographies and biographies of Mohammed Ali and a lot of other athletes as well, a very common theme is that they all believed in themselves. Mohammed Ali said, "Fake it till you make it" and "I am the greatest, I said that even before I knew I was."

Mary: I've certainly heard those before.

Jacob: He also said, "To be a great champion, you must believe you are the best. If you're not, pretend you are." And he became what he became.

Mary: Oh, fantastic.

Jacob: Speaking of Mohammed Ali, yet another quote that I really like – I actually had it printed on my wall – was "I hated every minute of training, but I said, **don't quit, suffer now and live the rest of your life as a champion."**

You might not enjoy studying for the LSAT, – I mean, hopefully you do so you won't have to suffer – but in any case, "suffer now" then live forever with your 99th percentile score.

Mary: Yeah. That quote is exactly what we're talking about. It's a very optimistic quote, like "Do the work, and you will be a champion." It's going to happen, not that it *might* happen, but *it will.*

Jacob: Right. Once again going back to our first question about motivation, actually, I think we might title this interview *LSAT Motivation* because there is just a lot of stuff about the subject. I would say as a motivator, you know, studying might also help you believe in yourself more. So, studying more can cause you to believe in yourself more, which can equal a better score, but it kind of comes from both sides. It comes from studying and also from believing in yourself. It can have a dual effect.

Mary: Yeah, absolutely, Jacob. That's very well put – I agree completely.

Jacob: Thank you. So, also on the blog, you talk about reading comprehension. I know that this is a touchy subject for many people, and I quote you from your blog, "If I had a dollar for every time I heard, 'Reading comprehension isn't something that I can improve on much, right?' I probably would have cable."

Mary: I think people think that by the time they've graduated from college, their reading skill level is pretty much set, and so they tend to be a little bit more skeptical about being able to improve on that section compared to other sections, which are just kind of inherently teachable – logic games, especially. Among our students, it kind of feels, looks and seems like a crossword puzzle, which is learnable. You know, everybody can learn how to do them.

Whereas with reading comprehension, everybody's like, "Gosh, I'm not a fast reader." They have this identity around their reading ability that's been established once they start LSAT studies. So, "I'm a bad reader", "I'm a slow reader."

Jacob: Which they don't have with logic games, for example.

Mary: Right, because they haven't really done logic games before. It's not like we grew up doing logic games in kindergarten, but with reading comprehension, we know we've been reading since kindergarten… So, people have this identity that they've structured around their reading level or reading ability.

All of this is to say that it's a common attitude to be a little more pessimistic about your ability to improve on reading comprehension. There's a couple of points here. Firstly, reading comprehension on the LSAT is its own thing. Like the rest of the test, it's quite literal. It's a logic test, after all, and so, learning what to read for, learning what the questions are going to test, can go a long way in improving your performance on that section. Learning to use the process of elimination can go a long way too. That's what I was describing before when I talked about working from wrong to right. It's the same thing, the process of elimination, and believe it or not, improving your actual reading comprehension skills is possible.

This goes back to what you and I were discussing before. It's about changing the way you think – making yourself a better reader. We're capable of doing that. It's just slower than learning to do a logic game. It's more arduous, but it is possible, just like it's possible to learn Spanish as an adult or learn any other language. It's not as easy as if you were four years old, but that doesn't mean it's impossible.

Jacob: Right, like you said, the logic games are something we've never done before. So, it's learning a new skill. We learn to deal with it somehow. Actually, a friend of mine works in a home, and he was sending some of the individuals for a trip to upstate New York. He had to match six individuals with six staff. Some staff could give certain medication to certain individuals, but not to other ones. Some staff were drivers, some were not, and he had to split them up into two vans so that each van would have a driver and the appropriate people to give medication to the appropriate individuals. I told him, "This is exactly like a logic game!"

Mary: It's a logic game. Yeah, it's exactly like a logic game.

Jacob: Yeah, the problem is that logic games are always solvable. Sometimes, real life logic games aren't solvable, but that's another problem.

I've heard from different attorneys that they said they've encountered situations where clients have come in and presented problems and dilemmas that were, in a way, a logic game. And they had to sit down, with their knowledge of the law, and figure out the rules of the logic game being the rules of the law and how the rules apply to their client's situation. That's practicing attorneys, but most people really don't encounter logic games in real life.

That being said, logic games really are a new skill, and you just learn it from scratch. Which is not the case with reading comprehension, as that is something that we already do. We already read – some of us more, some of us less – but it's technically something that we do already.

My opinion is that one of the things that is hard about the reading comprehension is that it's taking a skill that we already possess and making us do it differently. We already read, but when we read, we're only interested in the main point. We're not looking for, you know, the argument or inferences or what the author would agree with. Unless we're taking a test, why would we put so much energy into it?

Mary: Yeah, I see what you're saying, and I think what you're describing is probably a challenge for certain populations of people who are maybe already attentive readers, but now they have to be attentive in a different kind of way. I think an even more common challenge is that people just aren't, for lack of a better term, good readers. I mean, we skim read, like when we skim headlines. We don't focus, and that's a luxury you can't afford on the reading comprehension. You really have to be focused for three or four paragraphs, and that's hard. I mean, that's sort of even more of a general challenge – maintaining focus for that long. Does that make sense?

Jacob: Sure. It also makes sense to me for another reason, because I know a lot of people like that, and I talk about this in another interview in the book as well. I know people that do really well in logical reasoning and at the same time do very poorly on the reading comprehension, and based on what you say now, that makes sense because logical reasoning is a very short paragraph, and you can just focus for a minute twenty or so, and that you're okay with. Then, you take a deep breath, and you move onto the next one, and you are again okay with that.

But then, with the reading comprehension, you have to do three or four of the logical reasoning at one time and then do the questions all at one time. So, it just makes the focus aspect a lot more difficult.

Mary: I think this just kind of jumped out at me. Over time, in classes, we'll give people three minutes to read the passage, and if we have a discussion on what it's about, several people are going to have misread it, but when we break it down, paragraph by paragraph, okay, you have a minute, read this paragraph. Okay, let's talk about what the paragraph meant, people are much more likely to be accurate in describing what it was about.

So, their reading comprehension skills haven't changed in the 30 seconds between those two exercises. Of course, the whole is different from each of its pieces, but I do think, on some level, it's about the ability to maintain focus for one paragraph being a lot easier than the ability to maintain focus for four of them.

Jacob: Right, that makes sense. I think that if a student can see that to be an issue, then they can say, "Let me work on my focus rather than working on my reading comprehension skills, **because really my focus is the problem, not my reading**."

I think everybody is different. There's a lot of different problems people can have on this test that if people get a sense of what they might be having difficulties with, then they can at least address it and know what the problem is. It's not that they're not smart, or anything along those lines.

Mary: Yeah, and a final note on that. I don't mean to harp on too much, but I think one way to diagnose that, that being a focus problem, is that people find that they're having to reread passages

– like if they realize they just read the whole paragraph and they weren't at all in it and they just have no idea what they just read, so they have to reread the entire paragraph or a couple of sentences. **That's a sign that it's a focus issue.**

Jacob: Okay, awesome. So, I actually have two more questions for you, our last question being the most important, but I'll get to that in a bit. So my next question is, why are law schools so concerned with students' LSAT scores, and is it justified?

Mary: You know, the LSAT, the modern LSAT, was conceived almost 70 years ago or so[6], and it was just viewed along with several other criteria. It wasn't supposed to be the be-all-and-end-all of admissions. It still isn't. I mean, despite popular belief, it is just one of the criteria. It is given a lot of weight, and whether it's given too much weight, I fall into the camp that says, "No, it's not," for a couple of reasons, and we've already talked about some of them.

One, **it's democratizing in a way**. So, I think I mentioned a little while ago that it doesn't draw on external experience and knowledge. It's not testing me on my knowledge of Columbus or even about the founding fathers, or something where my level of education or my upbringing bears weight on my performance on the test. And you know, we can point to ways in which it does require a certain level of outside knowledge, but for the most part, it is a logic-based test. That's a democratizing thing. It's testing everybody, regardless of economic, ethnic and social background, and really putting us all on the same level playing field.

It's also a better apparent predictor of law school grades than GPA and, combined together, that's a better predictor than either of those two factors alone. So, it does seem to have some predictive

6 1948

value when it comes to performance in law school. It's not just a myth.

Then, okay, maybe this is a little soft and fuzzy, but it's just like what we were talking about earlier. As long as it carries so much weight, students preparing to enter law school are going to be motivated to study for it, to study well for it and to study hard for it. By doing so, they're actually teaching themselves to think more logically. It has this collateral benefit of making them better thinkers before they've even gone to law school and making them better law school students and ultimately better lawyers before they've even gone to law school. I'm not sure that would happen if it were not given so much weight. I'm not sure students would study as hard for it, and I think there is a more collateral benefit to teaching oneself to do well on the test.

Jacob: That's a very interesting take. **They're putting so much weight on it in order to encourage people to study because they know that will prepare them well.** That's a great take on the whole idea.

Mary: Right. It's like that myth where someone is motivated by the promise of this one thing, and then they get there and realize that's not what they actually wanted. Over the course of the journey, they've gained what the true benefit is. You know what I'm saying?

Jacob: Yeah, totally. What I always say is, there are plenty of books out there by a *single author* that offer ways to improve intelligence, ways to improve memory, ways to improve logical thinking, but then you have the LSAT, which is constructed by at least a few dozen people per administration. They invest millions of dollars every year in its development. So, it's not just a book by a PhD who has his or her own series of methods, but it's by a *lot of PhD's* who get a lot of money to really develop things that are very, very tight and extremely accurate.

Mary: Right Jacob. That's a really, really good point.

Jacob: We should be grateful for the LSAT and for the LSAC because they put so much work into it. If it was a test that wasn't so accurate, you could study for it, but this test is so tight. I constantly see people who get a certain score, then, without too much study in between, take another diagnostic and get the exact same score, which goes to show you how precise it is.

Mary: Right.

Jacob: There's no surprise 10 point increase just from, you know, drinking an extra cup of coffee or something like that. We should actually be grateful for that.

Mary: That's a really good point.

Jacob: So, that leads me to my last question. Last, but not least, Mary: **what is your number-one tip for students to improve on their LSAT score?**

Mary: I was going to say one thing, but I think I've already said it. I feel like that's an opportunity for me to get into something else! I was going to say: the longer you study, the better you're going to do. So you can't peak too soon. You don't get worse at the LSAT. Keep going and don't take it before you're ready.

Jacob: Mary, it's like with the law school rankings, some rankings rank the law schools as number one, number two, number three etc., and some rankings give you a few in the 3rd place, a few in the fourth place, and then jump to 7. We'll go with that ranking system for your tips.

Mary: So, let's do it that way, and I'm going to throw in another number one, which is to *turn off your headphones*. And I'm using that as a tip to encapsulate a whole attitude when it comes to studying, which is to find a quiet place where you're actually able to focus, instead of sabotaging yourself by leaving the music on and having a meal right next to you or drinking a beer while you're studying, or playing catch with your dog while you're doing a logic game.

I think that these are all really understandable things to do, or things like them are understandable, because, to be honest, one theory that I have is that the psychology behind this is that we're afraid that we're not going to be capable of focusing. So, we go ahead and prevent it in the first place so that we can blame it on, you know, the music, blame it on the TV being on in the background, blame it on the dog. If you remove all those distractions, we're just really left with our ability to focus in a quiet space, and that can be an intimidating thing, but it's also an essential thing. It can be incredibly empowering if you're able to do it, and you are able to do it. **It's just a matter of training yourself.**

If this is difficult for people, I tell them to start small, for example: commit to 10 minutes. "I'm going to do this game. I'm going to do this set of questions, and I'm not going to have any distractions at all. I'm going to turn my phone off. I'm going to turn it off. I'm going to turn it on silent and flip it over."

Jacob: Wow, you are very demanding.

Mary: It's very hard, isn't it? It is for me, too. I'm in the same camp. It's just so difficult for us to have so many methods of communication at our fingertips at all times. The best possible thing I think you can do for your LSAT study is to remove all these things. Remove all of those seductive tools of communication that are constantly at your fingertips and just focus on what you're doing, and it will pay off. The benefit of doing that can be tremendous.

Jacob: Wow, that does sound like a number-one tip, and I would in fact rank that higher than your other tip because the other things about studying longer can only really help if you're focused and concentrated. So, there's a concentration and focus guru. His name is Matt DiMaio. I saw him on YouTube, on a great video, talking about concentration. He asks, "What's the definition of concentration? Think of a laundry detergent that's concentrated. What happens if you add water to it? You dilute it."

So, adding the water is analogous to adding music in the background, to having your phone on your desk, like you said, or having your dog next to you, and it breaks your concentration, it dilutes it.

That's a great way to visualize it as you're putting music on: **you're diluting your concentration**. You're not helping yourself. Matt DiMaio also said it is okay if you play quiet classical music, and I agree with that, because you don't start snapping your fingers to classical music. If you're playing rock, pop or the like, you might stop studying. You start singing and you break your concentration. So, I think that really is a truly number one level tip for the LSAT. I also recommend students print it out.

"Turn off your headphones." Was that the exact quote, "Turn off your headphones?"

Mary: "Turn off your headphones." Yeah, exactly, and I'm with you on the soft classical music, except when it comes to taking full-length tests. The point of doing that is to simulate the real test conditions and, of course, you don't want to depend on the soft classical music. You want to be used to taking it when it's not there, when you're actually hearing, you know, you're hearing the siren go by, the dog barking outside, and the construction going on in the next block.

Jacob: Right, and the tapping of the pencils.

Mary: Yeah, exactly.

Jacob: They have those LSAT proctors, you know, the recorded ones, and they actually have them with noise in the background, common noises of people coughing and the like, to really get people to feel like they are in the actual test room.

Mary: Oh, that's great. I didn't know they had that. I love that.

Jacob: Yeah. So, that's something that people can look into as well.[7]

So, I think with that tip, *"Turn off your headphones"* I would want to finish with that because it's such a strong, powerful tip and I want people to remember that. You know, they say in court, when a lawyer is trying to make a point, the lawyer should stop after the point was made because if he or she keeps going, the jury might not be sure what the point is. I rest my case.

Mary: Right. Jacob, I don't know if you watch *Seinfeld,* but it's also like George Costanza, like that episode when he makes sure he leaves on a good joke. So, when he's made a good joke, he's out.

Jacob: I was just watching something yesterday about how Kramer decided that on every date he would finish with a jingle, and he would sing his name in a jingle so that the girl would remember him. I'm actually thinking of doing that myself.

Mary: I'm sure it's certainly memorable that way, right?

Jacob: So, again, Mary. Thank you so much. This has been a really incredible interview. I think that a lot of our brainstorming, as they say, two heads are better than one, brought out a lot of great ideas, and I think that's it's going to be very beneficial.

You tutor, and by the way, I highly recommend that people go to **ManhattanLSAT.com**, and they can sign up there for your tutoring

---

7 I personally recommend www.simugator.com.

if they're in New York, or for tutors in other places throughout the country. So go there right now!

I can imagine that students would probably not tend to get into such philosophical conversations with yourself or with another tutor for an hour because they probably just want to focus on the LSAT, but, then, there are these questions that they might have and they don't always have time or you may not always have time to answer them. So, here they are. Here you go. This is a great resource for students to read about other questions.

One of the reasons I really wanted to interview tutors like yourself, you know, top caliber tutors, is that there's so much misinformation on the internet. You go to all these blogs and forums, and they're kind of just talking with no coverage of what they're saying, no insurance to what they're saying. They don't really care if the person that's reading their tip is actually going to benefit from it. But someone like yourself, as a tutor, you care about your students.

So, when you answer questions like this about the LSAT, it's really coming out of a place of care. It's coming out of a place of concern for your students. So, you're going to make sure that your answers are true. I think this was very valuable and students will get a lot of knowledge from this interview.

Mary: I hope so.

Jacob: So, Mary, again, thank you so much.

Mary: My pleasure, it was really fun talking to you. And, yeah, I completely agree. This is a great project. I'm glad we got to get into some of the detail and the theory behind all of it. We just don't have time to have these conversations during tutoring because we're more focused on students' specific needs during those tutoring hours. So thanks for including me.

Jacob: Awesome. Thanks again, Mary.

Mary: Thank you, Jacob.

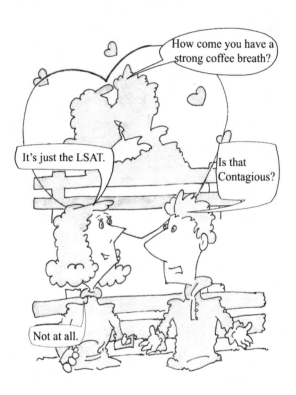

INTERVIEW WITH ROBERT FOJO

Jacob: Robert Fojo, of LSAT Freedom is a Harvard law school graduate. His understanding of the LSAT goes above and beyond and we are fortunate to have him here for an interview. Hello, Robert.

Robert: Hi, Jacob. How are you doing?

Jacob: I'm great. How are you this morning?

Robert: Very good.

Jacob: Thank you so much for joining us for this interview. I'm sure that our students and listeners will benefit a lot from it.

Robert: Absolutely. I'm glad to be here.

Jacob: I'd like to start with my first question for you this morning. What would you say is the **number one challenge for students on the LSAT**, and how can one improve, and get past, that one specific obstacle?

Robert: The number-one challenge for students on the LSAT is the logic that the exam tests students on. The exam requires students to understand and recognize an array of logical concepts, and that's a challenge to students who have never been exposed to logic before.

152

The way to improve that is actually by learning these principles in depth, understanding them, and being able to recognize them on the different types of questions that appear in the exam.

Jacob: Okay, that makes sense. So, why is the LSAT giving us those types of questions, specifically?

Robert: Well, because those concepts are useful. Although you may not learn these specific concepts in law school, law school is about legal reasoning and requires an understanding of logic in order to argue specific legal points and to recognize and challenge arguments from the opposing side. So, the LSAT asks these types of questions to force students to recognize these logical concepts because students will be using those concepts in law school, just in a different format. The concept of logical reasoning is deeply embedded in law, and it's an area that we are forced to learn, and have to understand, in order to succeed in law school.

Jacob: Okay. That makes sense. So, it's not just a test of general knowledge, but it's actually applicable to law school?

Robert: Absolutely.

Jacob: So that being said, how does one improve on their logical thinking and logical reasoning?

Robert: Well, it involves two steps, and this is the basis for the LSAT Freedom course. The first thing is that you actually have to learn and understand these principles. And the second step (the key step) is you need to practice real LSAT questions and understand how these concepts arise and are manifested in the questions. The best way to do that is by practicing with real questions over and over again, not looking for any types of keywords, phrases or any types of gimmicks.

You just need to sit down and do the work, and the more questions you practice, the more familiar you will become with the content. Then you actually begin to realize that a lot of the questions on the LSAT are really just restated and rephrased differently from exam to exam, but are essentially the same. You don't realize that until you've had a significant amount of exposure to the contents of the exam. So, that's the best way to overcome this obstacle. It's **understanding the principles first and foremost**, but **then applying them and extensively practicing with real questions.**

Jacob: So, you mentioned the idea of using real questions versus non-authentic LSAC published questions. Maybe you can elaborate on that?

Robert: Well, I think it's critical that you use real questions when you prepare for the LSAT. If you try to use made-up questions, it's only going to get you so far. It's likely not going to get you anywhere because these LSAT questions are put together by a group of people in a closed room somewhere, and no one really knows how they think! We can extract various ideas, thoughts and strategies based on the questions we look at, but we really don't know what they're going to come up with next.

So, the best way to prepare is by using the questions that they have actually prepared in the past. If you use made-up questions, no matter how hard someone tries to replicate the exam questions, it's still not the same thing. You're taking a risk by doing that. So you should try to focus on real past paper questions.

Jacob: Are more recent LSAT questions better to use than the older ones?

Robert: Yes, the more recent the better. Obviously, there's a limited amount of those, but it's better to use questions from the last several exams, even the latest 15-20 exams, than to use questions that were used 20+ years ago. Obviously, at the law school admission council, there's turnover, like anywhere else. It's best to look at, and use, questions that have been put together recently because they are more like the questions you are likely to face in your exam. Future exams are more likely to be put together by the same groups of people.

Jacob: So, I read on your blog once, "You know you're studying for the LSAT when you ask your girlfriend, 'What's your main point?'" So, does prepping for the LSAT really tend to carry over to real life?

Robert: Not to the extent that it makes you obnoxious! It does carry over, and it should carry over a little bit because it does promote clarity of thought. Whenever possible, we all engage in conversations and arguments, and hopefully they're just recent debates about whatever topic is at issue.

It helps to take what you're learning with the LSAT **and apply that in everyday conversation** once in a while, to see how you can improve the way you express a point, form an argument or recognize the flaw in someone else's argument. It's a helpful practice if it's there. I certainly encourage you to employ it. Although obviously, you don't want to annoy anyone.

Jacob: I found for myself, when I was studying for the LSAT, the common things that I would find were the assumptions people were making, and I would point those out. I could easily find people's assumptions which could weaken their argument.

Robert: That's right, and that's a perfect example. Assumptions are things that lots of people make when they're arguing a political point. People make assumptions all the time. It's helpful, and it's even fun, to identify what those assumptions are and how to challenge those arguments, if possible, because it is great practice for what is a very popular topic on the LSAT.

Jacob: I want to get, a little bit, into the nitty-gritty of LSAT preparation and pose some questions that I've gotten from students. One that I've got from quite a few people is about students who are quite successful on the logical reasoning section, and what I mean by 'quite successful' is scoring 22-23 questions correctly out of the usual 25-26. Many find that they then face an obstacle when it comes to reading comprehension. There seems to be some sort of paradox. If the difficulty with the reading comprehension is a comprehension issue, they wouldn't be able to do so well on the logical reasoning. Why can some people do so well on logical reasoning, yet at the same time do so poorly on the reading comprehension?

Robert: Well, because in logical reasoning each question involves a very limited amount of information. You're talking about just a few lines of content that you need to look at with respect to the question. Reading comprehension, on the other hand, involves 50-60 lines of a dense, uninteresting, dry and previously unseen passage.

It is absolutely brutal to read some of these passages. On top of that, what you need to do with reading comprehension is to be able to **distill that passage into two or three main points and then recall very specific information about the passage and draw very specific inferences about it.** So, those requirements are vastly different from a typical logical reasoning question. That's the main difference.

With reading comprehension, the key is to **read through it and set up guideposts for answering questions**. You have to quickly identify the main point or main idea of the passage. You need to identify any major concepts or individuals, any opinions that have been expressed, and those pieces of information will help you answer the questions that follow.

Jacob: Are there any crossovers between logical reasoning and reading comprehension regarding the tasks that they ask the test taker to perform?

Robert: Absolutely. The inference questions in the reading comprehension section are often very similar to some logical reasoning questions. So, the skills that you develop in answering logical reasoning questions do transfer over to reading comprehension, but the additional wild card with reading comprehension is that it involves, again, the comprehension of a significant amount of information before you start to apply those skills.

Jacob: My notion of the difference between logical reasoning and reading comprehension is that in logical reasoning, if you miss a point in the stimulus, you'll probably get the question wrong, especially if it's a crucial point that you missed. However, when you move on to the next question, your misunderstanding of the former question has absolutely nothing to do with this next one.

On reading comprehension, however, you don't have that. You have a whole passage, and you can misunderstand, like you said, the main idea, or you can misunderstand what the two sides of the dichotomy are or what the author's opinion is. And this misunderstanding can lead to you answering three or four questions incorrectly. Do you agree with that, Robert?

Robert: Absolutely. For example, in reading comprehension, you'll have one example that asks you the main point of the passage. You'll have another question that asks you what the author's purpose is. Those are obviously different questions, but if you miss one, you're probably going to miss the other one. You know, if you misunderstand what the main point of the passage is, you're probably going to also misunderstand what the author's purpose was in writing the passage.

So, I think that is an excellent point and it is critical that, in reading the passage, people **identify the specific, important pieces of**

information they can use to answer the question. In that way, they won't run into those traps.

Jacob: Can you elaborate on the difference between a main point question and an author's purpose question because that is actually something that I haven't heard a good explanation for?

Robert: Well, believe it or not, with the main point question, **you can usually find the main point specifically expressed in the passage**. Not all the time, but the majority of the time, the main point will be in the passage. You will be able to underline the actual main point, and it may even be self-contained in one sentence. It is more likely that it will be in two or three sentences in different parts of the passage, but it will be there. It doesn't require any logical deduction.

The question that asks you for the author's purpose, or the **author's primary purpose, actually requires you to make an inference**. You're drawing an inference from the information in the passage. So, that type of question actually requires that you read between the lines, so to speak, and try to infer, based on the information from the passage, what you think the author's purpose was in writing the passage.

That's the main difference between those two types of questions. A question that asks for the author's purpose is really more like a logical reasoning question than a main point question, or another question in reading comprehension that asks you for specific information that's explicitly included in the passage.

Jacob: Fantastic. In my next question **I want to address a very important issue**. I know of quite a few students who were scoring very highly on their practice exams. What I mean by high is in the high 170s, maybe even 180. They were getting almost every question right, even with excess time. The same students have later sat down to an official LSAT and come back with a score that was about 10 points lower than what they were scoring on the practice exams.

So, obviously, they're doing something in the practice exams that may be wrong. There's something that they are doing wrong, that doesn't help them make sure that the practice test is really indicative of what they're going to score on test day.

What are your thoughts about that? What are students doing wrong and how they can correct that?

Robert: Well, firstly, you need to look at how they are taking these practice exams. Are they actually taking them **under timed conditions**? Are they exactly replicating the conditions of exam day? That's the first thing to look at. If you take a practice exam, **you should try to mimic, as closely as possible, the conditions you'll experience on test day.** So, you should sit in a similar type of chair and desk. You should time yourself and adhere to the time. You should try to block out any types of distractions. It is often helpful to sit in a room with other people and to practice in that kind of environment because that's what exam day is all about.

Now, with respect to exam day, the first time you go and take an officially administered LSAT, even though you're trying to mimic that as much as you can when you take a practice test, you still can't do it completely. You're going to experience nerves, butterflies, all that stuff, and it's very difficult to replicate that elsewhere.

So, it may just be that, even if these students were doing everything right when they were taking the practice exams, on exam day itself, they blank. It happens. They're in the bathroom, and who knows what. Exam day itself is a very different animal. The best way to prevent any sort of meltdown on exam day is to **take as many exams**

and practice exams as possible under exam style conditions so that when you walk in that day, nothing's going to surprise you.

Jacob: Robert, would you recommend taking it a step further, for example: taking 30-minute sections? Like you said, there are those aspects that you can't mimic when you're at home or even at a library or public café. Maybe there are other ways you can induce stress, like perhaps lowering the time that you have to 30-32 minutes, and maybe that stress will equal the stress that you have on test day, even though it's caused by something else.

Robert: Sure. That's actually a very good point, Jacob. A little sports analogy: I played football in high school, and I remember our practices were harder than the actual games because they would run us into the ground and actually exhaust us in practice. Then, when you got to a game, it wasn't half as bad as the two-day practices.

So, I think that's a very good point. It may be helpful, especially if you're a very nervous person and you're going in on exam day. Sitting with all these nervous people around you is something that's going to create issues. It would be helpful to introduce additional stress to your practice in a very minor way. You don't want to go overboard here, but, yes, perhaps instead of 35 minutes, give yourself 30 minutes to complete the section. Then, on exam day, when you have those extra five minutes, it's almost a luxury, and you'll be glad that you have that extra time. It will be a welcomed rest. As opposed to letting the normal conditions affect you, you are now even more familiar with them. You are now more prepared for the environment.

It also really depends on the individual. I mean, I remember when I was in college, I knew someone who didn't do any preparation, went out and partied the night before, walked in on exam day, and got 176. Obviously, for him, he didn't need to employ a lot of these different techniques!

It really depends on what your needs are and what makes you stressed or nervous. You should do whatever you can to minimize those circumstances.

Jacob: I would say that for that friend of yours in college, then, maybe the partying *lowered* his score by four points.

Robert: Absolutely. He could have achieved a perfect score.

Jacob: That's actually an interesting point because he went out to party the night before, and he just took it so casually. Actually, I know a student right now who just got into the University of Chicago Law School. As an undergraduate, he was a big partier, and he really didn't take anything seriously. He got 174 on the LSAT with almost no studying.

I'm sure he studied the basics, but maybe the people that take it so at ease actually have an easier time. Maybe it's like catch-22. When you get so nervous at it, it's actually a disadvantage?

Robert: I completely agree with that. Although a lot of people don't like to hear this, at the end of the day, **it's really just a test score** and it's not the end of the world if you don't get into a top 10 law school. It's also not the end of the world if you don't end up becoming a lawyer. There are so many opportunities to succeed in life!

Focusing so heavily on the exam and essentially basing your entire life on one exam – it's going to create a lot of unneeded stress. Perhaps de-emphasizing all of that and reassuring yourself that this isn't the end of the world will actually help you decrease stress on exam day. So, I think that is a great point. [8]

Jacob: So that might have come out of our combined stories. Your story and my story, together, may have proven that point. So, it's something that we might want to look into more.

I wanted to go back to our first question about the main obstacle of the LSAT. You said it's mainly the logic and the difficulty in understanding it. Am I right in assuming this is because it's not something that we use on a daily basis?

If you haven't taken a course in Computer Sciences, for example, or something similar, which forces you to work on your logic, then logic seems very foreign. So, for somebody who's struggling on the LSAT, would you tell them to study more, study harder, or would you tell them to take a step back and study logic, since you know that's really the underlying skill that one needs?

Robert: Great question, Jacob. I think, in general, it all starts with logic. If you're going to take a logic course, I would recommend doing that because that provides a good introduction to that area of study. Of course, taking an LSAT course that teaches you those concepts is critical.

Then, as I stated earlier, sitting down and applying those concepts to real LSAT questions, and practicing with real LSAT questions as much as possible so that you gain familiarity with the questions on the exam, is extremely important. This will help you begin recognizing these concepts as they appear in whatever variations of the questions you come across.

Jacob: I think it's a very common concern that people have: how much time to put into actual LSAT studying and how much time

---

8 Let that idea help alleviate stress, which will ultimately raise your score. JE

to put into things that are related to LSAT studying. I know of a girl, in her mid-20s, who came to New York from Europe. She got a bachelor's degree, here in New York, but her English was still very poor. She sat down to take the LSAT, and she saw there was just no hope. She had no chance of getting the score she wanted.

So, this girl put her studying plans on hiatus, and she enrolled in an English class in a local college, and she really started working on her English. A year later, when she sat down to take the LSAT, she got 174.[9] So, she was obviously a very smart woman, it was just her English, (which might not be as important as logic is for native speakers), but for somebody who doesn't speak English, even the simple questions would be difficult, just because of the language barrier.

So, it just seems like there are a lot of people who have these LSAT-related problems, if you will, and they have to decide how much emphasis to put on those skills rather than just studying for the LSAT itself.

Robert: I agree with that. You know, unfortunately, the exam is in English. I believe, actually, in Puerto Rico, they're beginning, either with the next administration or next year at some point, a Spanish version of the exam.

Jacob: For Puerto Rican law schools?

Robert: Right. But I agree that there are certain extracurricular challenges for someone who doesn't speak the language or someone who has some other challenges before them. Unfortunately, yes, those people have to put in a little bit of extra work in order to achieve that baseline that other students are at before they can even begin focusing on what the exam actually tests.

---

9 Her tip is in this book. JE

Jacob: Okay. So, I think that would be beneficial for people to hear, because I feel that if somebody's studying for the LSAT and they're not getting the score that they're happy with, it can be extremely frustrating, especially after one enrolls in a course, and even takes some tutoring, only to find out that they're not improving or improving very little.

I think students would be happy to hear that maybe they need to take a step back and look at their whole situation, not just specifically at the logical reasoning or logic games. **They really have to assess their academic abilities in general, and that might be a way for them to achieve their goals.**

So, let's make a shift towards logic games. What is the key component to understanding and doing well on the games? Also, Robert, you mentioned that repetition can really help a person understand and perfect that mindset needed to excel on logical reasoning. What would your advice be as far as it comes to logic games?

Robert: With respect to logic games, the advice is very similar. The key thing with logic games is to understand how to set them up, and in order to do that you need to identify what kinds of games you're dealing with. So, if it's a grouping game or an ordering game, there's a certain way to set up these types of games. **The more you practice, the more familiar you become with them**. You can determine more quickly how to set them up, and once you begin to set them up, you identify what the variables are, where all the spaces need to go and what rules you need to follow.

You can then begin to deduct additional rules and restrictions that are not expressed in the game itself. Once you complete that setup, you can begin answering the questions, but it all starts with that set up. That setup can make or break how quickly you go through the game. If you spend too much time on one game when you have three other ones to do, you're running into time constraints. So, the setup is critical, and finding, I don't want to say shortcuts, but if you can determine by the process of inference, additional rules and restrictions and start predicting how certain pieces are going to be grouped together or how the order is going to play out, then, potentially, you can identify two possible scenarios for your game.

You can narrow it down to something like that. That dramatically increases the speed with which you can run through those five, six or seven questions for that particular game. So, **it's all in the setup** of the logic games.

Jacob: You said before that the main obstacle for students in the LSAT is the comprehension of general logic. Would that be the same for the logic games?

Robert: Absolutely. There is a certain basis of information that you need to know for logic games. Conditional reasoning is a very critical area to learn for the logic games section, and there are a lot of 'if...then' statements that you can apply to the logic games section. So, logic is an important component of that section, just like all the other sections.

Jacob: Right. So it sounds as though the LSAT is on a spectrum, if you will – it's a spectrum of logic. It comes out, as far as game set ups and formal logic. Then it comes to logical reasoning, where it's actual text and it's more about understanding logic in context. It sounds like it's all the same test, they just test it in different ways.

Robert: Absolutely, and they really get into it thoroughly in the logical reasoning. You kind of get a taste of it with logic games and the reading comprehension. Logical reasoning is the two sections that really delve into the specific types of logical contexts and logical fallacies that you need to understand for this test.

Jacob: You also mentioned before that **logical reasoning is at the**

heart of the law. Now, it makes sense why the LSAC is testing people on logical reasoning – to see how well they'll do in law school. But why are they testing logic games? I know it's a common question. A lot of people ask it. People ask why do we need to do logic games to get into law school? So I wanted to get your take on it.

Robert: It's an interesting question. I view it as a very crisp way to test very specific logical concepts, and some people find it fun! If you get the set up right, you can breeze through the games and get all the questions right. So, it's an opportunity for students to get a perfect score on the section if they know how to approach these games. I view the logic games section as, perhaps, the easiest section on the LSAT. A lot of people may not agree with me, but it's an opportunity to score a lot of points very quickly.

Jacob: How does that tie into law school? I mean, they're not doing logic games in law school.

Robert: No, but it does test specific logical principles. I think I mentioned conditional reasoning. You have to learn logic for that specific section. You do apply certain concepts in that section, and by learning and applying those concepts, you obviously understand them further. You will be applying those concepts in legal reasoning later on, both in law school and in your career.

So, it does have value. It does have a use. It's just administered in a different, fun way, but it does have value later on.

Jacob: I can tie that into something I learned in a class on how to conduct interviews. One of the ways they teach to take an interview is to give an abstract question. An example of that type of question would be the following: you're the mayor of a city and there's a train coming into the city with 50 sick people. If they get into town, the entire town is going to be infected and die. So, do you blow up the train of 50 people and save the 100,000 people in the town, or do you let them come in and take the passive approach?

Obviously, hopefully, nobody's going to be in that situation in the future. It, for sure, has nothing to do with the job. You're interviewing someone for an office job – they're not a mayor! However, it's an abstract question and it's interesting to see how the person reacts and to see what approach they would take. One person will make a face and identify how hard it is to answer a question like that. A person like that, you can see they have more compassion in their heart. Even though they know the right answer, if there is a right answer, they take that approach.

An interviewee with a colder approach would say, "Well, obviously, you blow up the train." It's testing a certain quality or trait, but without going there directly. So, in a way, that's what I feel the LSAT is doing with logic.

Robert: Right. If you look at the LSAT, the entire exam is just a set of abstract questions, and the point of the exam is to assess a student's understanding of logical concepts. The only way to do that is by presenting students with over 100 intangible questions in order to test their understanding of those concepts. So, logic games are just one specific way of presenting those abstract questions, and I think it's a very crisp and clear way to test some of those concepts.

So, the entire exam, really, is just an abstract format for testing an individual's understanding of those logical principles.

Jacob: So, Robert, in your LSAT course – LSAT Freedom – you teach the basic methods, but you also review a lot of LSATs in depth. I know there are a lot of courses out there that teach the fundamentals, teach the basics and the logic that you're talking about, but really don't go over more than four or five LSATs altogether. You actually go into, I believe, 17 or 18 LSATs, question by question. Why do you take this approach?

Robert: Well, it's what's unique about our approach, and we believe it's critical for doing well in the exam. Learning and understanding these logical concepts is obviously not enough. The best way to really advance your learning and understanding of these concepts is, I think the phrase is, **"learning by doing."** We all learn best by actually doing something. You learn how to play basketball by going out there and taking a ball and learning how to shoot, not just by sitting and reading a book about basketball. We learn by doing whatever trade, craft or task you want to learn.

With the LSAT, the best way to learn these principles is by actually sitting down and practicing real questions. We provide detailed explanations of questions on 17 or 18 LSATs, and the way you recognize these different concepts, as they appear in the exam, is by seeing them and actually practicing the questions and seeing how these concepts manifest themselves in the question. Doing that over and over again is obviously a little time-consuming, **but doing well on this exam does require some work**.

The more you work through these questions, the more you become familiar with the content and the more you can start predicting what kind of concept each question is testing and you start recognizing these concepts. That's how you succeed on this exam.

Jacob: I know it's a more expensive approach as well because you have to license the questions, you have to pay the LSAC fees, etc., but with that, you guys are actually not charging more than most, I believe?

Robert: Yeah, not really! Other courses actually provide all of the exams, which they're paying royalties for. So, that's actually more expensive, but you're not going to go through 68-69 exams. You're actually going to sit down and do the exams, but that's why we don't provide all of them. We try to go for the most-recent ones in depth and in detail, and if you go through all those exams, you go through all our explanations, you should be able to do well on the test.

Jacob: So, Robert, *last but not least*, if there was one tip that you would leave for our listeners and readers as far as LSAT preparation goes, **what would that one tip be?**

Robert: Well, there's really no secret sauce or silver bullet when it comes to doing well on the LSAT. **You just need to sit down and put in the work and practice.** I think our approach is the best approach for preparing for the exam: learning the logic and sitting down and working through as many questions as possible so you can recognize these concepts in whatever form or variation they appear.

Jacob: In other words, you mentioned that your tip would be to take a systematic approach, like you said, learning the logic and then seeing how it applies to the LSAT. Your first part of the answer, to me, was a tip as well, in that *there is no secret sauce*. I think that, in itself, is a number one tip because I know a lot of students, and I might be guilty of this myself, who waste time surfing the internet, looking for one thing that's going to change your whole preparation around and just boost your score by 10 points automatically.

I think even though most people understand, logically, that can't really exist, I think there is a tendency for people to at least look for it and believe that if they buy this book, sign up to this course or hire that tutor, then they'll improve drastically with minimum effort. I think that the one tip that they need is exactly what you just said: that there is no one tip. So, just stop wasting your time with that, and crack open the books. That in itself is an awesome tip.

Robert: Yeah. Well, Jacob, society tends to glamorize success. We prop all these billionaires and the Mark Zuckerbergs' or the Bill Gates', but no one ever focuses on the work those billionaires put in order to develop their company and the products that have made them so successful. Believe it or not, they actually put in a lot of work. Bill Gates built computers in his garage. He labored away and built that company. Zuckerberg put a lot of work into that website.

To succeed at anything, we need to put in the work. **There is no secret sauce to success**. It requires hard work. You need to work smart, but it does require you to put in the effort.

Jacob: Right, I think that's a good point. They say that if you want to be like Bill Gates when he's 40, you have to be like Bill Gates when he's 20. You can't just be the person at the end result.

When it comes to famous talent, you see the end result. You see their built body. **You see their strength and their speed and everything, but what you don't see is the effort that they put into it**. What happens in the ring – they win a big boxing match. I'm not sure how long a boxing match takes, but however long that is, that's just a fraction of what they put in. That's just the end result.

So, that being said, I personally recommend for everybody to go to LSATFreedom.com and look at the curriculum. I think they're offering, now, 101 tips on the LSAT. I think that's a good place to start. Sign up for the newsletter. Get the LSAT Freedom course, because I think it's a sure way to success and, just like Robert mentioned, remember that there's no magic potion, there's no pill. If there's a pill, it's called studying. And when you study, you have to study the right way. You can't just pick up a book and hope that you'll understand logic games.

I remember when I first saw logic games. I said to myself, 'I wonder if there are any books that explain this stuff?' It turns out there are lots of books, and a lot of courses, but like I said, if there is a pill, it's studying hard. It's taking, like you said, a strategic approach – learning the fundamentals and studying actual tests.

So, Robert, thank you so much for being with us.

Robert: Absolutely. It was my pleasure, and thank you very much for the recommendation and for your time.

Jacob: Thank you again, Robert. Have a great rest of the day.

Robert: You too, Jacob. Thanks a lot.

Interview with Steve Schwartz

Jacob: Steve is an LSAT expert and the famous LSAT blogger at lsatblog.blogspot.com, which has become the number one LSAT blog online. He is a Columbia law school graduate and a cool guy, so we are extra lucky to have him here today for an interview. Hello, Steve!

Steve: Hi, Jacob. How are you doing?

Jacob: I'm great. How are you today?

Steve: I'm great, thanks.

Jacob: So, let's get to it. My first question is about the logic games. The logic games are probably the most feared subject on the LSAT. Yet many students are able to achieve a perfect score on the logic games. So, why are they the most feared and how does this transformation occur?

Steve: Well, it happens because logic games, for most test takers, are really the lowest hanging group in terms of their preparation. If students are typically unfamiliar with games, they seem very boring. Unless you went to a nerd math camp over the summer, chances are you haven't seen many problems like this before.

172

The reading comprehension – well, you've been doing reading comprehension on the SAT and the ACT. You've had it in high school. Logical reasoning, while you may not have had anything to do like it, in terms of analyzing arguments, it's really something involving lots of reading, which is familiar to most test takers. Games are a bit more mathematical and symbolic. Most test takers don't have a background in problems of that nature. So, that's why they are the most feared.

The transformation to a perfect section comes from realizing that although games might seem mathematical, they don't really involve any kind of math. They involve a limited set of skills that you can refine and ultimately perfect, simply by becoming familiar with the patterns that are tested. You can become familiar with these patterns **by doing lots and lots of LSAT games**. So, the transformation involves doing lots of LSAT games and then learning the methods to attack those games, learning efficient diagramming techniques and the common formats and formulas that the logic game section uses.

I've found in my analysis that there are a number of common formats and formulas that the LSAT logic games use, in terms of how you can go about making inferences. So, I went through many of the old exams and I grouped together games that seemed similar to each other. I found that there were certain types of grouping games, specifically in-and-out games (also known as selection games) where the process by which test takers could make inferences would be extremely similar from game to game.

So, if you've done one of these older games, you would, then, be well-prepared to make inferences in one of the newer games **without having to reinvent the wheel** on the spot. So, a lot of scoring a perfect section comes from being time efficient, which, in turn, comes from recognizing those patterns from the previously administered exams.

Jacob: That might be easier said than done!

Steve: Yeah, well, it's going to take a lot of work. It involves a lot of practice.

Jacob: Right. I know, on your blog, you have video explanations of every single logic game, I think, from the 30s and on, if I'm correct? I've viewed them myself.

Steve: Yeah. Right now, I have from test 29 and up. Eventually, I'm going to add the older ones as well.

Jacob: So, basically, you're saying if one can go over a certain amount of logic games and memorize the inferences and the feel of the game, questions and the right and wrong answers and just get into the flow and into the pattern, they'll be able to do well? Like you said, a lot of them repeat themselves – not exactly, but in some form.

Steve: Yeah. On the one hand, the LSAT is lazy in that they're simply taking old games and dressing them up with a new topic. Of course, they're not really lazy, and these games are not completely identical to each other. They're just incredibly similar, and I suspect that the reason the LSAT likes to use this same format over and over again is because they test the skills that the LSAT wants to test. Test takers who are more diligent in their studying may pick up on those patterns.

You're always going to have people who do very little studying. They just walk into a bookstore, pick up the first book off the shelf, and they consider that adequate preparation without really doing thorough research beforehand in terms of what materials are best and that sort of thing. It takes a lot of work. It's not really memorizing, though. It's just **about becoming familiar with those formats through repetition**.

Jacob: Okay. So, with that being said, there's a lot of games out there. There's at least 70 something LSATs with A, B, C. How many games would a student need to learn in order to be proficient on a new LSAT?

Steve: Well, everyone's different, of course. Everyone has different levels of aptitude. So I can't give a one-size-fits-all answer. I would say that, probably, the most recent 30-40 exams worth of games would be more than sufficient for the vast majority of people. But this involves not just doing them once, but doing them and **redoing them**. Maybe not redoing all of them, but maybe redoing some of them. I would say using maybe 20 exams worth of games builds a strong foundation, and then using another 15-20 exams worth of games to complete, either individual-timed sections or full-length timed exams.

Jacob: Okay, that's great advice. So that being said, maybe the games are something that shouldn't be feared?

Steve: No, I don't think they are something that *should* be feared. I think it's something that's kind of a blessing in disguise because you are able to perfect your skills on this section since there's a limit to the kind of format and game types that they use. So, you're far more able to perfect your work here than on either of the other sections.

Jacob: That's great. So, my next question is a question that I hear from a lot of people, and I promised that I would ask you this one. Some students get to a place where they're consistently scoring a correct amount of answers on any of the three sections on the LSAT, and after more than one test, maybe five or six tests, they're still scoring 15 or 20 out of 25 questions on the logical reasoning and 15 or 20 out of 23 on the logic games, whatever the number might be. ***How do they break that barrier and get a few more points?***

Steve: Well, my answer to that would have to vary from section to section. Someone who's already scoring 20 on games, close to perfect but not quite perfect – those extra points are simply going to come from **more repetition and better time management**. One example of something that test takers should do on logic games, in my opinion, is: **don't go through all five answer choices on any given question.** Once you've already found the proof and you've proven that something is the answer, whether it *could* be true or it *must* be true or any variation on one of those, you need to take the answer and move on.

You have to trust your diagram and your inferences. That's something that could help you save time on games when you already have the fundamentals down. You get better at it by learning the method and then applying and reapplying them to be more and more automatic every time.

With logical reasoning, someone who's already scoring around 20, again, they already have the fundamentals down, most likely. So, I would suggest that if they can't find any particular weak areas in terms of a particular question type that gives them trouble, then it could be down to time management issues. **Think about getting through the 10 questions more quickly** so you have a time bank built up to give yourself ample time for those more difficult questions. So, if you get through the first 10 questions in 10-12 minutes, you'll then have more than the average amount of time per question to attack the more difficult ones later in the section when you need it.

You know, double checking and triple checking question number 3 on LR isn't going to make that answer any more correct. You've already got that question right, most likely. You need to save that time and devote it to something that would actually benefit you.

Jacob: That's very beneficial information.

Steve: With the reading comprehension, not getting too bogged down in the passage and not spending more than three minutes on the passage is something that will allow you adequate time to solve the associated questions. And that's my big time management tip for reading comprehension.

Don't try to learn or memorize all the details in the passage. Chances are you're not going to, especially if it's a topic with which you're unfamiliar. So, you're going to want to go back to those details later, when you have the detail-oriented questions. Just focus more on getting down the main idea, the primary purpose, and anything else that you believe it's likely they will ask about in the question.

Jacob: Right, that makes sense. So, in your tutoring, do you encounter students like that who get stuck on a certain score?

Steve: I do have students like this, and my biggest recommendation is to really focus on the logic games. You know, going from 20 to 23 on games... those three questions there are a lot easier to achieve than going from 20 to 23 on LR, as LR is a far more complicated section (in my opinion) because you have a variety of question types and you have a million different methods of reasoning, whereas games are more regular and standard. There are fewer types of games and I find that, for more students, they're far more able to perfect their scores there.

In reading comprehension, there's only one section of reading in the LSAT, and it's fairly difficult to improve upon that level. I find that, of course, if you're getting 20 correct on reading comprehension, that's still seven or eight questions on games. So, there's still a significant amount of work to do there as well.

Jacob: So, a lot of it comes down to also doing the math or, better yet, **being a strategic test taker**. If you're missing 10 questions on each section on logical reasoning, that's 20 questions altogether, but if you're missing 10 questions on logic games, that's only 10 questions.[10]

Steve: Right. I think games are perfectible. So, it's worth a lot of time there, but if you had 10 wrong on reading comprehension versus 10 wrong on either of the other two LRs, I'd say focus on LRs. Any change you make in LR, in terms of your standing, will likely be doubled.

Jacob: Right, and that's great advice. In your courses on the LSAT, I know you cover subjects about *high scorer habits*. Why is it so important to learn about high scorer habits, or about habits in general?

Steve: Well, I find that people who do really well on the LSAT – people who are getting in the 170s – have something I call the "LSAT mindset." Some people are born with it – they're natural-born geniuses. Then you have other people **who intentionally prepare for the LSAT and eventually acquire that kind of mindset**. Myself? I would fall in the latter group. I wasn't born this way. I used to be normal. I eventually developed these reasoning abilities through studying the LSAT.

I find that most people taking my course and reading my blog… most of them are not geniuses. Most of them are simply people who are smart. They have great aptitude, but they are still gaining new skills and information. So, developing that mindset is not only something that can help you with the LSAT, but also with life in general. We're focused on the LSAT here, so we're supposed to talk about that. That's why I call it the LSAT mindset or the LSAT mentality.

People who score in the 170s, they tend to develop a similar approach to reading arguments, reading the passages and, of course,

---

10 There are two sections of logical reasoning and one section of logic games. JE

to attacking the games. That approach comes from being critical of arguments, being skeptical of them, not taking things at face value, considering alternative causes for any result and alternative explanations for any conclusions. It's about really developing that attention to detail, not just looking at things in a general way and skipping over important modifiers or qualifying statements. You have to really get an appreciation **for the nuances** of what you're reading. So, what I'm suggesting now is really applying more to reasoning and reading comprehension where you have a lot of language involved.

Then, with games, it's about taking what they give you and not only applying it, but, at the same time, reading carefully and not reversing conditional statements, for example. Having this general approach (and you can gain it, of course, through doing lots and lots of the LSAT problems and reading anything critically that you encounter in real life) will mean you're much better suited to attack any LSAT question you come across, whether it seems familiar at first or not. If you simply apply a technique that you learned from somebody else, you're not going to be able to attack that as well when you're faced with an unfamiliar problem on test day, and it may throw you off due to general test day stress and that sort of thing.

So, it's really important to learn the habits of high scorers so that you can adopt them, rather than just simply knowing how to diagram this kind of rule when you come across it.

Jacob: In another interview in this book, I spoke about the skills of the LSAT carrying over to law school, and it sounds like there are some specific skills in the LSAT that do carry over. We also talked about the idea of how studying for the LSAT improves the skills that you need for the LSAT and will also help you in law school itself, because those skills are needed in law school. So, my question for you is not about the *skills* of the LSAT, but about the *habits* of the high scorers. **Will those habits also carry over to law school and help a person succeed in that environment?**

Steve: I absolutely believe that they would. I have a hard time seeing how they wouldn't! I think that learning to read more critically and developing an appreciation for detail on what you read – I certainly believe that would carry over to law school. I haven't been to law school myself, as I've said, but I did take a law school-style course in undergrad that even included the Socratic Method used by the professor.

We read a lot of Supreme Court cases, and they are complicated. They're wordy. I mean, they're written in a difficult, high level style. So, being able to dissect cases that you have to read in school and being able to appreciate the nuance of contracts is incredibly important. I think that's one reason the LSAT is so big on trying to trick you with lots of little details and synonyms and things that might seem like synonyms, but actually aren't. It's because if you are a lawyer, and a client comes to you and gives you a contract to read over, and you don't catch something really important in that contract, your client's going to be in big trouble. You might be guilty of negligence for not seeing that detail in the contract. So, being able to read carefully is an incredibly important skill for a lawyer to have, and, of course, law school, to some extent, is training you to be a lawyer, so you would certainly apply those skills there as well.

Jacob: Awesome. That's another benefit of studying for the LSAT. I also mentioned this in another interview: I think I saw it on your blog, as well, but I also saw it when it came out in the Wall Street Journal, about the correlation between studying for the LSAT and improving intelligence, which was an awesome motivator.

Now, this adds to my list of motivators to study for the LSAT, and that is that you will acquire the correct habits that will help you in law school, I guess. It is fair to say that you acquire the right habits if you get a higher score? Is that a fair assumption?

Steve: Absolutely, absolutely. That can go a long way to improving ones score. So, if you're doing better on each of the sections, I would certainly say that suggests that you're acquiring the correct mindset. Of course, no one particular prep score necessarily indicates where you stand, but if you see your average prep score starting to rise gradually over time, and then significantly, I would say, chances are, you've acquired that mindset.

I also think you'll see if you've acquired that mindset if you start seeing in everyday life that you're being more critical and skeptical, for example: when your friends, significant other, or family members are making general real-world arguments, and you start seeing flaws in their arguments. Of course, you don't want to start pointing them out all the time – then people are going to get sick of you – but if you start noticing those things in your head, it's a really good thing.

Jacob: Right. That makes sense. So, that brings me to another question, and I hear a lot of the same thing from different students, especially from students who take a hiatus on their studying. They study over the summer, then they realize that they're not ready. So they wait for another few months, and they decide to defer law school about a year or so. Then they come back to studying, and the main question is: where do they start? Do they start from the beginning again, or do they find wherever their bookmark was and continue from there? How do they approach that?

So, my question to you, about the habits, is if somebody is trying to break the barrier of a certain score, perhaps they can step back and say, "Let me evaluate my habits. Maybe my habits are the problem," and if not, they need to study more. They need to change one small element that will make the small change.

Steve: I think the mindset and the habits are really important, but that's a general perception. That's a general way to think about things. I think, if you've developed it, you're not likely to lose it because it's such a general framework for looking at the world, and it becomes such a deeply ingrained habit that I'm not sure if someone will lose that.

I would say that if someone took a long time off from studying and is feeling kind of rusty, and they need to get back into it, I think the way to get back into it would just be by doing actual LSAT problems from each of the three sections and figuring out where their weak areas are. Not actually picking up where they left off. They may need to backtrack a little bit, but I think, overall, the issue with taking time off and getting back into it is just that you got so focused on other aspects of your life that you forget the LSAT-specific strategies that you need to do well.

Jacob: Okay, okay. So, yes. That was my presumption, but I'm taking your expertise on that subject. That being said, I know you mentioned the habit of reading detail, but could you tell us another one of the habits, maybe, that high scorers have which helps them score high as well?

Steve: Yes, sure. I think that a degree of skepticism is really important. So, for example, a logical reasoning stimulus claims that one thing guarantees another one. You may not necessarily have to predict what that specific alternative is, but it's keeping an open mind that there are potential alternatives out there in the real world that exist. So, one of those alternatives could weaken their supposed explanation.

Jacob: Okay. So, skepticism would be good. So, in short, you're saying that this is an important for LSAT takers?

Steve: Yeah. Absolutely.

Jacob: Okay. I mean, a lot of the time it's frowned upon in the real world, so to speak, when people are too skeptical of certain things, and, also, there's often a problem when there are habits we need in the LSAT that are not, like you said, skepticism or arguing with everything, looking for weakeners or stuff like that – those are things that might not come naturally because of the way you're brought up. All of a sudden, you need to be clear cut. Everything needs to be black and white, and you can't play around with things and be nice, so to speak. So, that might be a challenge for some people.

Steve: Yeah, sure. I think that people in the real world aren't skeptical enough. That's my opinion, but I think it's a good habit to acquire, in general. I think it's important.

Jacob: Right, right. I mean, of course, then you have the opposite. You have conspiracy theorists that take everything that ever happened and say, "No. It didn't happen," but they don't normally have adequate proof for that.

Steve: Yeah. Of course, the amount of evidence is incredibly important and I think, in general, it's about not being too certain. So, the conspiracy theorists might be convinced of their particular theory, but they're just not sure about people who accept the status quo. There are people who, on the one hand, they're too certain of conspiracy. Then there are people who are convinced of what the majority of people think as well.

Skepticism is not just about believing in your personal or conspiracy theory. It's about recognizing the limited evidence that we have and just how restricted that evidence actually is. Does the evidence in front of us actually give us any explanation at all? Alternatively, maybe we don't have enough evidence from which to draw a conclusion.

Jacob: Right, right, right.

Steve: Not being too certain.

Jacob: Exactly, yeah. It reminds me of the movie Zero Dark Thirty, where they were hunting for Bin Laden, and the actress playing Maya, she's the girl in the CIA that found Bin Laden based off their intelligence. When they're discussing whether, for certain, Bin Laden is in that compound, they're giving percentages of how much they believe he's there. They all give 60%, 70%. When they get to Maya, she says 100%. Then, she says, "I know that certainly freaks you out, so 95%, but it's 100%."

Steve: So, that's a good example. You can go back to Socrates and Shakespeare. Both Socrates and Shakespeare said things regarding this. Translations are always difficult, but Socrates said something along the lines of, "I know nothing except the fact of my ignorance." Shakespeare said, "The fool doths to think he is wise, but the wise man knows himself to be a fool." So, basically, the smarter you get or the better your reasoning ability gets, the more you realize how little it is you actually know, or how little it is that you can actually conclude, based on the information that you see in the world or the evidence that's presented to you.

Jacob: Exactly. So, that takes me to my next question, and this might be a hard question. I know that a tutor of your caliber probably won't have a problem with it, but when I heard this question, I was at a loss for words. I know a few students who are scoring close to 180 on their practice exams, and I was specifically thinking of their example because you can't get higher than 180. Then, on the real LSAT, they actually plummeted around 10 points. They went from around 180 to 170-169, around there. How could this happen? How did this happen to those students, and how can one make sure that the scores they're getting on their practice exams are a real indicator of what they will get on their actual exam?

Steve: Sure. That's a great question. I hear about things like this happening all the time. People are scoring close to 180 and then dropping 10 points. There are people all across the spectrum who have what I would call a 'test day drop', and there are a variety of reasons this can happen.

There are two main reasons I can think of. Firstly: nerves and stress. The other big reason is not practicing under real test day conditions. Regarding nerves and stress, some people find stress actually boosts their score. There's positive stress, which lets people shine. Then, there are other people who kind of fall apart under stress, and that's a big topic. I'm not an expert on stress, in general, but one thing I've heard that can help people with stress reduction or anxiety reduction is meditation, which I talked about on my blog. It's something that a lot of people are interested in, and it applies to the LSAT. So, meditation, any kind of stress reduction technique, could be helpful to make test day just seem like another practice test.

Another way to reduce test day stress would be to practice under conditions similar to those you will be experiencing on test day, as much as you can, to make your actual exam simply nothing more than just another practice test, another one in the long line of exams you've already taken. Okay, just talking about practicing under real conditions, a big part of that is strictly timing yourself, not taking a break in the middle of a section to go get a drink or going to the bathroom and pausing the clock while you do that. If you want to go do that, the clock's going to be running. It's like on test day, or you can wait until the break.

Also, taking five section exams rather than just four section exams is a good idea because on test day you will have that experimental section, and you need to factor that into your studying so that you will be accustomed to developing that level of endurance that you're going to have to deal with on test day. So, don't do only four sections on your practices and then do five on test day and be like, "Geez, I was so tired by the last section." You have to be practicing under those realistic conditions. Otherwise, your scores could be falsely inflated when you're getting those super-high scores, and then you'll see that drop.

Jacob: Would you recommend, by the way, doing the essay as well? I know it's not scored and it's also the end, so it won't make you any more tired, but as far as the essay, would you recommend doing that once in a while?

Steve: I don't really think it's worth devoting time to. There's no reason why you should take time away from your actual LSAT studying. Just focus on the essay, the sample. I mean, you should certainly look at it at least once. It's one short thing they ask about, but, in terms of importance, it pales in comparison to the actual scored sections.

Jacob: The reason why I mentioned people are scoring 180 is because if you're scoring a 155, it might be safe to assume that your actual test will be 3 or 4 points lower than that, but with a 180, you can't get 183. So, how can you make sure that your score stays up there? So, I think that's great advice. What you said is to practice under real conditions and alleviate stress as much as possible.

I mentioned this elsewhere, but we all know about the fight-and-flight reactions, right? When you get anxious or nervous, the blood from your brain flows to your arms and legs so that you can fight or flight, and that can actually lower your IQ by 10 points which is a big deal because that's not the response that you need on a test. If you confront a grizzly bear or a lion, that's what you need, but if you're on a test, you want the blood to stay up in your brain so that you can focus as much as possible.

So, I think that's great, again. I know I read on your blog, also, about the meditation. I think that's actually a really big deal. I don't think people realize how much test anxiety can lower your score, and if we might put even 1% of what we're actually studying into meditation, or any other method that could lower stress, I think it's well worth it.

Steve: Absolutely. I agree completely. I have a blog on meditation I did a few months ago, and I'm going to do another one, specifically about the stress anxiety aspect of it. When I was talking about meditation on the blog, I was actually talking about meditation as it applies to developing focus and concentration, helping you avoid getting distracted when you have to read those really dense, and often boring, passages or logical reasoning stimuli, but I think it has a number of other benefits too. It doesn't even have to be something spiritual. It could just be something that you do for practical reasons for you to just gain the benefits of it.

Jacob: That actually brings us to my next question that I prepared from before, actually. The question is on your blog. You previously talked about meditation as a way of improving LSAT performance, and there are other ideas that you also have on your blog, such as playing the famous dueling back games to improve logic games, as well as other ideas that are intended to improve the underlying skills to the LSAT. So, how much time should one dedicate to these non-directive ways of improving the LSAT versus the traditional LSAT studying?

Steve: Sure, it's a great question. Meditation, in particular, has such a variety of benefits that I think even just devoting five minutes to it a day could really help a lot. Of course, if you don't like it, don't do it, but at least give it a shot. Five minutes a day – I would certainly recommend that for anyone preparing for the LSAT.

Actually, the other thing I think is duel n back. I think that it remains to be seen how much that would help, but I know a lot of people like to play Sudoku as a way to try to help with their logic game performance. That's kind of like duel n back. I think those can certainly help. They might have some loose relationship to LSAT logic games or LSAT reasoning, in terms of making inferences, but I wouldn't count Sudoku or duel n back as LSAT study time.

So, don't say, "I'm not going to bother doing LSAT logic games because I did dual n back today, or "I did dueling back for 20 minutes. That's 20 minutes of LSAT studying." I think that dual n back or Sudoku or other kinds of non-LSAT puzzles. I would say those are something that could be a supplement to studying or something you do to take a break from studying, or maybe if you're taking the LSAT a year or two from now and you want to casually get into studying without doing something as focused as actual LSAT problems, these can be a good way to dip your feet in the water without getting too stressed or too focused on this. However, I would say that they don't really count as studying.

The best way to improve your LSAT score is to do actual LSAT problems, read LSAT-specific materials or watch LSAT-specific videos.

Jacob: Those two, Sudoku and dual n back, are probably the most famous as far as the LSAT students talk about, but it's exactly like you said. You shouldn't count it as LSAT study time.

What I would recommend is if you have a certain amount of time that you want to study, let's say you've decided to study 2-3 hours a day, do those two or three hours first. Then you can play Sudoku as much as you want, but don't do it first because you might get distracted. Then you'll be tempted to think, "Well, I did some Sudoku. So, I'm okay."

Steve: Yeah, sure. That's a fine approach in terms of integrating those alternative, loosely related LSAT things into your day or week. I think sometimes Sudoku is a great thing to do. It's a great way to do some studying during your commute to work if you're taking the train or the bus, maybe, but you don't have enough focus during your commute to actually look at LSAT-specific things.

Jacob: Now, that's a great tip. So, as far as a schedule goes, we're talking about if you have two or three hours, but how would you recommend splitting up the studying of the three sections of the LSAT? So, we have three sections. Sometimes, you're better at one section, but not as good on the other section.

We talked a little bit before about the fact that logical reasoning has almost double the questions than the other two sections. That being said, let's say for somebody that's starting out and isn't yet sure if they're much better in the reading comprehension or the logic games., just as a way to start, how would you recommend splitting up the three sections?

Steve: Yeah, sure. That's a topic that I've thought a lot about. I've made a million different LSAT study schedules for all different periods of time, whether you're studying for one month, two months, all the way to seven months. I've also made both general week-by-week versions, you know: what you do over the course of a week with your studies, and I've also made much more specific day-by-day LSAT schedules that tell you exactly what to do on each day over the course of your studying, even including things like exactly which pages in various prep books to read and which specific LSAT problems to complete.

So, in terms of how to go about your studying, I've thought a lot about it. In terms of breaking up the sections, I would say, for most people, the best place to start is the logic games just because, as we discussed at the beginning today, logic games are the most feared, but they're also the most perfectible. So, games are scary. They're the lowest hanging group. Starting there can lead to massive gains rather quickly and really boost your confidence a lot, and because you want to perfect this section more than any other, you're going to want to complete a lot of LSAT games and really make sure you familiarize yourself with something that is so foreign at first. So, I'd say: start with logic games. Focus on learning the basics of those.

Then, once you learn the fundamentals of games, then I would say, start on logical reasoning, since logical reasoning is the next most foreign and complicated section of the LSAT, whereas reading comprehension is a bit more familiar to most test takers. So, start with games. Then cycle in logical reasoning work while you still do logic games every week to stay fresh. Then, with the majority of your time, you can focus on logical reasoning each week. Then, finally, once you learn the basics of that, finally introduce reading comprehension while still maintaining the other two sections so that you don't get rusty. Finally, once you learn the fundamentals of all three sections, then focus on doing timed sections for each and full-length test exam leading up to test day.

Jacob: Okay. In a nutshell, that's a lot of great information, and, like you said, you have those wonderful study guide schedules which I think are probably the most important things someone could buy, besides actual study guides, because you're juggling three sections. In some ways they are similar, but in many ways, they are very distinct. So, maybe getting better at logical reasoning will help you somewhat in reading comprehension, but the connection between getting better with logic games probably won't be as clear in improving your reading comprehension. Maybe in the long term, just dealing with logic and dealing with inferences like that, but we're talking a few months. It's not really going to make a difference.

I struggled with it myself and a lot of people I know have struggled with it. "What do I do today?" They go into the library. They have all their books, but it's like, "What today?" You know? So, I've also heard, in relation to other subjects too: just start. If you don't know what to do, it's just going to make you overwhelmed. Just start. Studying something is better than not studying at all.

So, that's one approach, I guess, but having an actual guide that they can purchase and print out, mark things off on and make notes – I just think that's a lot of help. I think it's a lot of guidance; a good price for a lot of guidance!

Steve: Absolutely. I see what you're saying. Thank you.

Jacob: Right. So, I have a last question, but I actually have a surprise last question. So, we'll do two questions. What would your number-one tip be on how to improve and study for the LSAT?

Steve: My number-one tip, just to keep thing simple, would be to make sure that you're practicing on copies of originally-released actual LSAT prep tests. Don't use fake questions that you got from some random book in the bookstore and make sure they're really official LSAT questions. Also make sure that after you've completed the problems, you review those problems in detail. Don't just complete a problem and say, "Okay, I got this score. I'm happy," or "I got this score, and I'm sad. Time to move on to another exam."

Don't just do that after your exam and expect to see results. Of course, you will familiarize yourself with the questions a little bit, but you'll really see some significant gains once you start analyzing your thought processes in detail, thinking about what you did when you were thinking about those problems and completing them the first time around. Then, make sure that you're learning why the correct answer choices are what they are and why the LSAT is including those tempting wrong answer choices.

So, do real LSATs and review them in detail afterwards.

Jacob: Okay, that sounds like you know something when you hear it. I don't know if that's true, or what the saying is, but anyway, I'll say it again. Yeah, that sounds to me like a number-one tip. That's number one material right there. Okay, so my surprise last question for you, Steve, is, for example: I have a friend who taught the LSAT about a year before she actually took it. She took a practice exam.

She got some high scores. Then, she was teaching for a whole year, and she took the LSAT and got 180.

Steve: Oh, wow.

Jacob: Yeah. I think she was getting in the high 160s or something to begin with, but she really attributed her success of 180 to teaching. She had one of the most difficult LSATs with a very hard logic game with destinations, airplanes, traveling, something like that. So, she really attributed her "easy" 180 to teaching. So, I know that you're a tutor. You write a lot about the LSAT, and I know when you're writing on the Internet, it's written in blood, not in ink, so to speak.

So, you don't have to define what you say. You really have to make sure everything is exact, make sure everything flows, there's no contradictions to other blog entries you've previously written. You really have a lot of experience that most people don't have, especially people who just study, take the LSAT, and forget about it.

So, all that being said, what have you learned? How has the depth of your understanding of the LSAT changed from the day you started or when you started to teach, until now, with the blogs and tutoring?

Steve: Sure, it's a great question. I would say, basically, over the years I've really developed more and more of an appreciation for just how complex this exam is and how much work goes into creating it. I've interviewed a former writer of actual LSAT questions a number of times on the blog and speaking with him, just the way he speaks and the way he writes, it's so refined. I see that similarity in how the LSAT itself is written.

They devote such an obsessive attention to detail and the wording and everything they create. So, I've noticed that more and more. At one point, I started writing my own LSAT-style logic games. I've written a number of them. They're on the blog, and with the process of learning to write my own games, I really developed more of an appreciation for LSAC's efforts in writing games.

When I started writing my own games, I found that it would take me a full day to write one game, from start to finish, in terms of the scenario, the rules, the inferences associated, and all the questions and correct answer choices, wrong answer choices, etc. There's a lot of thought that goes into creating wrong answer choices for all three sections! So I have noticed things like that over time as I developed different tasks for myself that I wanted to do for the blog, whether it was writing the games, writing logical reasoning explanations or creating videos for the blog.

Every little project I've worked on that's related to the blog has taught me something new about just how deep the rabbit hole really goes when it comes to this exam. I've tutored other exams in the past, like the SAT and GMAT, and I've found that the LSAT is really deeper, more complex and more deserving of respect than any of the other exams that I've come across. I find that the people who really do best on this exam, the people who get the highest scores, really develop a real appreciation for this exam. It's hard to hate something once you become really good at it, and once you understand it well.

I find that people who are scoring really low, like in the 140s, they'll say things like, "Oh, the LSAT's dumb. It doesn't test anything worth knowing. It's a risk. Why do they have this?" Once you start getting better at it and once you master it, you'll say, "This exam is really awesome. I want to teach it. I want to write about it. I want to know more about it. It's really worthy of respect and study."

Jacob: Wow, that's an awesome answer, Steve, and who but you can give an answer like that? I think it's also very encouraging – the fact that there is something to appreciate about it, the fact that it is possible to even love the test and to really appreciate it. I mentioned before the fact that the LSAT can improve your intelligence, and we mentioned this in another interview. I think that in itself is something that you can appreciate because they're sitting there, developing the LSAT in a way that will improve your intelligence, whether it's intended or not, but regardless, it will improve your intelligence.

So be thankful because people pay a lot of money for websites that offer different brain games and things like that. Here, you have a book that you have to study and you have the extra benefit of getting smarter. Again, who doesn't want to be smarter than they already are?

Steve: Oh, absolutely. I completely agree. I found that, for myself, going from when I started with this exam until today, I found that the way that I think, speak and write – it's all become more refined and specific. I think I speak a lot more deliberately than I did when I first started with this. People have noticed it: the way I speak and the way I think. I've noticed the way I analyze what other people say, what other people write, and I really do everything earlier, that LSAT mindset of really thinking critically and skeptically and developing attention to detail that other people think and speak and write.

It's really something that can help you in life, as long as you're not a jerk about it to other people.

Jacob: Right, and that's a good caveat. So, Steve I really want to thank you. This has really been an awesome interview. I think that we've covered some great information. One of my goals for these interviews was to have questions that aren't easily answered, that anybody can look up on Wikipedia, you know, how many sections on the LSAT and stuff like that. My goal is really to drive information from people like yourself, who have the answers, but

I don't want to waste your time or other people's time with really simple questions.

I think the information that we covered tonight was really awesome. So, I want to encourage the readers and the listeners of this interview to head over to LSATblog.blogspot.com, and you will see a lot of Steve's recent blogs. They're pretty often – I think you post there once a week?

Steve: Yeah. At the moment, I'm doing about once a week.

Jacob: Right, right. What's important about a blog, you know, is that things change. Over the years, we've had new questions added in logic games. In 2007, they started the comparative reading in reading comprehension. So, things have changed. Things get updated.

Even the fact, I think there was a hurricane a few years ago, and they cancelled. So, the LSAT thing was updating, but I saw the update on your website. Why do I need to go anywhere else?

Steve: Yeah.

Jacob: So, you know, you stay updated for us, and you let us know through your blog, which is awesome. Like I said, I mean, it's just like a whole library of blogs that you have on all subjects. It's not just the subject of the LSAT, but there's stuff about test day, admissions. There's stuff about the law school diaries from a lot of prospective students. It's just so much information, like I said.

Also, one of the biggest assets of your blog is the free videos, which are incredible! I know a lot of people use them because any logic game that they're having trouble with, they look up LSATblog. blogspot.com, and they find the answer. Besides looking for an answer, something they can't figure out, my advice when people tell me about logic games is: even if you're getting all of them right, you might not be doing things as efficiently as you could be. Even though you're getting them right, you could be doing them in a way that is wasting time. If you're not doing things efficiently, you might make a mistake on a different logic game.

So, seeing the videos that you have, Steve, will help people, not just with the games that they're having trouble with, but even games that they're okay at, just to get a little bit more efficient and refine those small inferences and make sure they're doing things the right way. Like I said, that's a huge thing. Of course, like we went through before, there's three different courses: the logic games, the reading comprehension and the logical reasoning and study guide. It's just a whole library of LSAT stuff.

Again, thank you so much for joining us.

Steve: Well, thank you, Jacob. It's been a real pleasure. These questions have been very thought-provoking and definitely got me thinking a lot as well.

Parting Words

NOW THAT YOU'VE SEEN THE amazing tips and interviews, it's time to put them to use. On the one hand, the LSAT is a means to get you into law school. On the other hand, you can also regard the exam as something inside of you that needs to be perfected. Humans are logical beings. Society is based on logic, as are our laws, justice system, and, of course, our arguments.

If logic is something so basic and important, wouldn't it make sense to be familiar and fluent in it?

Then you have the LSAT's reading aspect. I would argue that reading is just as important to life as logic. If we couldn't read, we'd have to post traffic cops at every stop sign and have someone yell the words on the sign at each exit on the freeway. You'd need a person at every aisle in the grocery store to tell shoppers about the nutritional value of every item on the shelf (based on a 2,000-calorie diet, of course).

Here again, I wonder, if reading is so vital to life, shouldn't we become *really good at it*?

I know what you're thinking. What about the logic games? How does that fit into your hypothesis?

In my opinion, the logic games test and strengthen our ability to make sense of a given situation. For instance, if you see an ancient Egyptian mummy walking down the street, you'd probably freak out. But if it's Halloween, you wouldn't think twice about it. Why? *Because the scenario follows the rules.* The rule is, that on Halloween, you're not crazy to walk around dressed as a mummy or a witch. On other days of the year, this might be problematic (unless you live in New York).

So if understanding the rules of life is so important, wouldn't that understanding be a skill you want to master?

And might as well perfect these skills before law school, right?

Always, Jacob